Gabler Theses

In der Schriftenreihe „Gabler Theses“ erscheinen ausgewählte, englischsprachige Doktorarbeiten, die an renommierten Hochschulen in Deutschland, Österreich und der Schweiz entstanden sind. Die Arbeiten behandeln aktuelle Themen der Wirtschaftswissenschaften und vermitteln innovative Beiträge für Wissenschaft und Praxis. Informationen zum Einreichungsvorgang und eine Übersicht unserer Publikationsangebote finden Sie hier.

Lili Jassemi

Global Virtual Teams & Trust

How Leadership Can Build Trust and Enhance Team Performance

Springer Gabler

Lili Jassemi
Munich, Germany

Leipzig (Germany), HHL Leipzig Graduate School of Management, Dissertation, 2022

ISSN 2731-3220 ISSN 2731-3239 (electronic)
Gabler Theses
ISBN 978-3-658-41851-9 ISBN 978-3-658-41852-6 (eBook)
https://doi.org/10.1007/978-3-658-41852-6

This Springer Gabler imprint is published by the registered company Springer Fachmedien Wiesbaden GmbH, part of Springer Nature.
The registered company address is: Abraham-Lincoln-Str. 46, 65189 Wiesbaden, Germany

Dedicated to my beloved father
(1938–2021) & to my dear mother

Foreword

In the last two decades, the megatrends of globalization and digitalization have rapidly increased global and virtual teamwork. This was reinforced once again by the pandemic. But even without this 'accelerator,' the possibility of global virtual cooperation offers numerous advantages that make the increase in its existence plausible.

At the same time, challenges emerge that threaten successful cooperation in such teams. One of the most important challenges is building and maintaining trust between team members. This is especially true in intercultural teams because there may be different perceptions about routine procedures, ways of dealing with things, and more, which can lead to misunderstandings and, as a result, conflicts.

With mutual trust, such misunderstandings and conflicts can be solved quickly and constructively or even avoided in advance. However, teamwork takes place primarily or even exclusively virtually. In that case, conflict management of this kind may be made more difficult, for example, because the opportunities for getting to know each other better in informal conversations—such as in canteens, coffee hall encounters, or tea kitchens—are much more limited. And familiarity breeds trust.

But how can you create the conditions for successful collaboration in global virtual teams? Dr. Jassemi addresses this issue in this book. She argues that the working conditions of global, virtual teams can impede a crucial prerequisite for successful cooperation: sufficient reliability that other team members do not exploit their advantages—and, more generally: vulnerabilities—in situations in which they could derive short-term benefits from them.

Accordingly, the authors highlight two insights: (1) Building and maintaining trust is based primarily on the shared recognition of the moral norm to do no (illegitimate) harm. (2) Leadership is central in promoting such a shared understanding as the basis for trusting cooperation.

It is worth emphasizing how Dr.Jassemi successfully applies a simple but substantial scheme for her argumentation: The connection between values, reality, and investments. Because of its simplicity, this scheme can have an orienting function even for managers, both for themselves and for their core task of motivating others to invest in value-creating (collaborative) work, but at the same time to pay attention to self-limitations that are an expression of mutual respect—and thus make trust possible.

These insights are more critical today than ever before. And so it is to be wished that this book will find many readers.

Prof. Dr. Andreas Suchanek

What the Burn taught me about leadership

My Ph.D. journey on agile leadership, cooperation, and trust, as well as my professional experience within the art world, which accumulated in the organization of a camp and music stage at Afrikaburn in the Tankwa desert in South Africa in 2019, a vast community gathering with various forms of playful interactions, art, and performances, made it once again clear to me that humans learn, live and create best in trust-based, inclusive playful communities, especially if the circumstances are challenging and constantly changing, in short in modern *tribes.*

Based on these insights, I merged the best of both worlds; cutting-edge academic research and practical wisdom about agility, cooperation, and community-building, and co-founded *Avantgardist Institut.* As a mission-driven interdisciplinary research and educational platform, we support leaders, teams, and organizations to build trust journeys for effective, long-lasting cooperation and optimal performance.

Adapted to the reality of a digital, diverse, and decentralized future of work and education, this book's contents and methods have been incorporated into our D^3 SKILLZ and D^3 TRUST Journey. Through our D^3 Experiential Learning Method, which uses unique human and digital networks through playful interactions and embodied cognition, we allow individuals to acquire the necessary mindset, skills, and values to build D^3 Tribes to thrive in a fast-paced world. Inspired by Prof. Dr. Andreas Suchanek, our Avantgardist slogan is "*Invest in teams. Invest in trust!*".

Grateful to these wonderful human beings

Without my family, friends, and other supporters' tremendous support, care, and love, I would not have accomplished this work. Thank you to all of you wonderful human beings!

My work is dedicated to my dear father, Parviz Jassemi, who inspired this research, Mr. Do No Harm, in words and action. I further thank my caring and loving mother Akram Hosseini-K., my brave lion-woman (shir-zan) sister Azadeh Jassemi, my honest and truthful brother-in-law and co-founder Antimo Di Donato, and my wise and kind-hearted brother Constantin Schmidt-Thomé for supporting me throughout all these years in pursuing my dreams. Thank you for being my family!

I am specifically grateful to my dear doctoral supervisors, Prof. Dr. Andreas Suchanek and Prof. Dr. Tobias Dauth, as well as the academic institutions, the HHL Leipzig Graduate School of Business, and the Wittenberg Center for Global Ethics, where I had the honor to study, learn and grow. Moreover, thanks to Dr. Lisa Schmalzried, Dr. Martin von Brook, Waldemar Hötte, and Mario Klimpke. Furthermore, I would like to thank Karl and Dr. Katrin Schlecht, as well as the Karl Schlecht Stiftung, for funding my research and still tremendously supporting me in spreading the ideas of this book beyond the academic realm into business practice; special thanks to my great supporters Dr. Jonathan Keir, Katharina Springwald and Dr. Kira Eghbal-Azar.

A big thank you to my outstanding co-founders and friends, Dr. Felix Wittke and Gabriel Mayrhofer, as well as to our advisors, co-creators, and partners, Prof. Dr. Marlen Komorowski-Albert, Jonas Albert, Prof. Dr. Thomas Kühn, Monica Wimmer, Eva Kaczor, Kiana Mardi, Joshua Bundschu, Joscha Raue, Prof. Dr. Christian Neuhäuser, Milaad Rajai, Santa Meyer-Nandi, Ashkan Allaf, Dr. Susannah Belcher, Henrike Luszick, David Lieber, Kenneth Mikkelsen, Ewald Klassen, Ruth Harley, Lukas Gautlitz, and Nanook Hinz.

Further thanks to Milena Bürki, Caren Döpke, Chiara Heinzelmann, Eleonora Kopitzsch, Yvonne Ernicke, Magdalena Wallkamm, Bettina Dircks, Greta Voss, Ramin Shirdel, Joerg Geier, Bettina and Klaus Schmidt-Thomé, Romana Fuchs-Mayrhofer and Peter Mayrhofer, my Mexican family Sarah, Aurelio and Cristobal Lopez and Pam Corr, Stephan von Perger, Luiza Maldonado, Max Pfadenhauer, Julia Denike, Johanna Demant, Angelina Grauman and the whole Cobracabana tribe!

You are the very reason the contents of this book have become my life's vocation.

Thank you *soul tribe*!

Dr. Lili Jassemi

Contents

Abbreviations

BCT	Behavioural Complexity Theory
CMC	Computer-meditated communication
e.g.	for example (Latin: exempli gratia)
et al.	and others (Latin: et alii / et aliae)
etc.	and similar other things (Latin: et cetera)
GVL	Global virtual leadership
GVT	Global virtual team
HRM	human resource management
i.e.	that is that is / in other words (Latin: id est)
ICT	Information and communication technology
MM	Mental model
SMM	Shared (team) mental model
VT	Virtual team
VUCA	Acronym for volatile, uncertain, complex, ambiguous

1 Introduction

Within the past decade (global), virtual teams have become integral to organizations in all sectors. This trend has been further accelerated since the emergence of the global COVID-19 pandemic in early 2020. Even though the employment of (global) virtual teams has opened up numerous new opportunities and benefits for companies and employees alike, the performance of these teams is often an issue due to a lack of trust. Trust is a necessary condition for successful interactions and requires adequate leadership. This thesis will demonstrate how (global) virtual leadership can build and sustain trust in (global) virtual teams for effective cooperation and enhanced performance.

The introductory remarks of this chapter explain the context of the problem statement of this thesis as well as the theoretical and practical relevance of the investigation of (global) virtual leadership and trust-building. Following this, the research question and the hypothesis are formulated, the methodology is presented, and the content and structure of the thesis are brought forward.

1.1 Global Virtual Teams and Their Societal Importance

With the beginning of the Information Age, network organizations have emerged as a new form of organizational structure, and (global) virtual teams (VTs) are the latest buzzword in the corporate circles of the 21st century (Junea, 2015).

Since the 1970 s, several trends have pathed the way for the rise of virtual work related to communication, enhanced methods for information transfer, and technological development (Weiler Reynolds & Bibby, 2017). Ever since, new communication and technological advancements have fuelled the rise of VTs (Powers, 2018). Also defined as the peopleware of the 21st century (Lipnack & Stamps, 1999), VTs are marked by spatial, temporal, and structural dispersion

L. Jassemi, *Global Virtual Teams & Trust*, Gabler Theses,
https://doi.org/10.1007/978-3-658-41852-6_1

and make the most use of information and communication technologies (ICT) for communication and cooperation with little to no face-to-face encounter with their team members or their leaders (O'Leary & Cummings, 2007). Furthermore, due to the globalization of the economy and the internationalization of companies, all kinds of businesses ranging from big corporations to SMEs have started employing a diverse workforce that works remotely in different parts of the world. Thus, many organizations today employ global virtual teams (GVTs) as an integral part of their organizational structure in all sectors (Anthony, 2020).[1]

Marked by the socio-cultural diversity of its team members (Kayworth & Leidner, 2000), GVTs are growing in prevalence as they are of the utmost importance to maintaining the increasingly globalized social and economic infrastructure (Morrison-Smith & Ruiz, 2020, p. 1). GVTs combine the advantages of socio-culturally diverse and virtual teams and thus offer various benefits for companies and employees alike (2.3.1). Amongst others, the employment of GVTs allows organizations to assert themselves in international competition by recruiting talents worldwide and making use of their expert knowledge, regardless of their physical location (Kayworth & Leidner, 2000), while offering expertise and service-intense activities (Fajen, 2018, p. 71; Townsend et al., 1998). Moreover, previous research has shown that thanks to the socio-cultural diversity of GVTs, organizations can make use of their team members' local knowledge and sensitivity to better respond to client requests or for the creation of new products while having a multitude of perspectives that enhance innovation and allow better problem-solving (Fajen, 2018, p. 272). In line with previous VT research, employees working in GVTs have a better work-life balance and flexibility than in traditional teamwork. Thus, GVT work can positively impact employees' emotional and psychological well-being and, ultimately, their performance (Cascio, 2000; Fajen, 2018). According to industry and policy leaders is, virtual work one of the biggest drivers of transformation in the workplace (Powers, 2018, p. 7).

The employment of GVTs has seen a massive rise since the global COVID-19 pandemic in the first quarter of 2020 (Anthony, 2020). 80% of global corporate remote work policies have shifted to virtual and mixed forms of virtual team collaboration since the global pandemic. Many organizations say this shift to virtual teamwork will likely be permanent (Meluso et al., 2020). Therefore, the successful employment of GVTs is one of the most critical future entrepreneurial

[1] While subsection 2.1.1 will define the concept of global, subsection 2.1.2 will define the concept of virtual teams. Thus, consequently, a working definition of global virtual teams (GVTs) will be given at the end of subsection 2.1.2. As for matters of understanding, the concept of global adds the dimension of socio-cultural diversity of team members to the overall definition of virtual teams.

challenges. Organizations that do not use these teams effectively may be fighting an uphill battle in a global, competitive, and rapidly changing environment (Duarte & Tennant, 1999, p. 2). Thus, as GVTs are becoming more and more relevant for policy and industry as they respond to an increasingly globalized and digitalized world, organizations should provide the necessary framework conditions for effective (global) virtual collaboration.

1.2 Research Problem and Relevance: Global Virtual Teams and Trust

However, to be able to use the diverse opportunities of this form of teamwork, in line with previous VT research, this thesis argues that good global virtual leadership (GVL) is needed to successfully meet the new challenges that come with the employment of GVTs (Fajen, 2018; Hoch & Kozlowski, 2014; Kayworth & Leidner, 2002; Lipnack & Stamps, 1999; Zigurs, 2003). Due to their spatial, temporal, and structural dispersion (O'Leary & Cummings, 2007), GVTs face numerous challenges related to communication, the use of technology and socio-cultural differences (Morrison-Smith & Ruiz, 2020). These challenges often result in miscommunication, misunderstandings, and various conflicts (2.2.2), thus undermining cooperation and performance (2.2.3).

VT research agrees that the successful leadership of GVTs requires GVL to fulfill a variety of diverse roles and demanding tasks while having specific virtual leadership competencies and personality traits that need substantial practice, ongoing training, and experience to ensure effective cooperation and thus performance in GVTs (Fajen, 2018, pp. 315–322) (2.3.2). Similar to traditional leadership, GVL needs to set clear common goals, develop strategies for the team, assign tasks and roles, and control team performance, amongst others (Fajen, 2018, p. 171; Jarvenpaa & Leidner, 1999; Jawadi, 2013). Like traditional leadership, GVL is in large part responsible for the efficiency and success of its team. However, research has shown that GVL faces additional challenges that require extra effort and time, especially concerning accommodating cooperation issues that can arise due to the socio-cultural differences of team members (Holmstrom et al., 2006). Thus, successful GVL needs to take on various novel employee and task-related roles to respond to the socio-emotional needs of individual team members (Fajen, 2018). In line with that, GVL must encourage motivated behavior and self-efficacy in its team while promoting team identity, cohesion, and friendships among team members. GVL is further required to mitigate conflicts to enhance collaboration (Ford et al., 2017, p. 7, Fajen, 2018). Generally speaking, GVL must understand how to guide and lead digitally properly (Fajen, 2018, p. 5).

Prior VT literature agrees that the main challenge and most important task for GVL are building and sustaining trust (2.3.3). Performance in GVTs require effective cooperation between GVT members and GVL alike, and previous VT research largely agrees that trust is a fundamental condition for successful interactions (Ford et al., 2017; Jarvenpaa & Leidner, 1999) (2.3.3, 3.1.1). Previous research has shown that many GVTs fail due to lack of trust leading to miscommunication, misunderstandings, and conflicts undermining team performance (2.2.3, 2.3.3, 3.1.1). As GVTs present unique challenges due to their spatial, temporal, and structural dispersion and, more specifically, due to socio-cultural differences of the team members (2.2.2), the trust-building process presents itself as equally more challenging than in co-located teams (Hacker et al., 2019; Morrison-Smith & Ruiz, 2020) (2.3.3, 3.2.1, 3.2.2, 3.2.3).

Previous VT literature from the realm of management sciences has introduced strategies to build and sustain trust in GVTs on a general level focusing on the promotion of face-face-face encounters, social information exchange, and regular interactions (Ford et al., 2017; Jarvenpaa & Leidner, 1999). Furthermore, GVL is advised to create communication methods that further trust (Jawadi, 2013). Moreover, VT authors have focused on GVL characteristics and leadership traits that promote trust in GVTs based on conceptual research (Flavian et al., 2019) and empirical studies (Fajen, 2018). Even though previous research gives exciting insights into the trust-building process in GVTs, so far, none of the previous research has elucidated trust-building in GVTs from a business ethical perspective which explicitly deals with the formation of trust relationships and expectations. Consequently, the business ethical concept of the golden rule's do no harm dimension, and more specifically, the ethical focal point do no (illegitimate) harm that allows forming mutual trust expectations (Suchanek, 2015; Suchanek & Entschew, 2018), has not been introduced within a VT context yet.

Thus, the societal and academic relevance of the research topic of successful GVL leads to the following research question: How can GVL actively promote trust in socio-culturally diverse GVTs and form mutual trust expectations that ultimately lead to effective cooperation and performance?

This thesis answers the research question by introducing a business ethical perspective on trust in teams while bringing together VT research key findings on trust, GVT, and the role of GVL. This thesis hypothesizes that successful GVL for effective cooperation and performance in GVTs can build trust by investing in trust through realizing the ethical focal point do no (illegitimate) harm.

GVL can do so by applying the business ethical model of good leadership for trust (Suchanek, 2019), which offers orientation points for its behavior and GVT members (3.3).

1.3 Thesis: Content and Structure

The object of this thesis is the leadership of GVTs for trust in an organizational context. This thesis draws upon VT literature from management sciences and, more significantly, from intercultural management research with regards to culture and leadership, social sciences such as sociology and (social) psychology, as well as communication and information sciences amongst others (Fajen, 2018; Ford et al., 2017; Gibson & Cohen, 2003; Holmstrom et al., 2006; Jarvenpaa & Leidner, 1999). This thesis uses a conceptual framework and merges previous VT research based on trust and leadership in GVTs, as well as insights from business ethics on trust in teams (Suchanek, 2015, 2020; Suchanek & Entschew, 2018). This thesis elucidates the context in which trust-building in GVTs occurs while summarizing the variables influencing trust in GVTs. Regarding that, the impact of socio-cultural differences and the role of GVL on trust in GVTs find particular relevance. In line with that, this thesis elucidates how trust relationships are formed, especially with regard to the socio-culturally diversity of a team, and how GVL can influence the process of aligning mutual trust expectations thanks to the ethical focal point do no (illegitimate) harm. Moreover, this thesis applies the business ethical model of good leadership (Suchanek, 2019), and the ethical focal point is to do no (illegitimate) harm in a case illustration based on the company Think-it (Think-it, 2022). For that matter, a tailor-made leadership seminar was created and executed in June 2021 (Avantgardist Institut, 2021).

This thesis is mainly based on relevant key VT research till 2019, as well as some individual papers on the matter of trust, GVL, and GVTs from 2020, 2021, and 2022 in line with the novel research element of this thesis with regards to trust relationships and expectations in GVTs. As the emergence of the global pandemic since the first quarter of 2020 has marked a decisive point with regards to involuntary and unprepared employment of any kind of virtual work in organizations, research with regards to GVL, GVT, and trust relationships and expectations during or after the global pandemic will not be taken into account. This particular context of the global pandemic regarding organizational restructuring requires more research and data points that this thesis will not provide.

The content of this thesis is structured as follows: Chapter 2 will introduce the state of the art on GVTs, GVL, and trust. First, in 2.1, the definition of the subject matter of global virtual leadership and teams is given with regards to 2.1.1 the concepts of global, 2.1.2 virtual teams, 2.1.3 virtuality and dimensions of dispersion, and 2.1.4 leadership. Second, in subchapter 2.2, a summary of GVTs in practice is given with regards to 2.2.1 the rise and benefits of GVTs, 2.2.2 the specific challenges in GVTs related to communication, the use of technology and socio-cultural distance, and finally 2.2.3 the effects of these challenges on cooperation and performance in GVTs. Third, in subchapter 2.3, the subject matter of GVL will be elucidated with regards to 2.3.1 the challenges of GVL and mitigation strategies, 2.3.2 the specific leadership competencies and related roles of GVL, and 2.3.3 trust a fundamental condition for leading GVTs effectively. Fourth, in subchapter 2.4, this thesis's research gap and contribution are brought forward.

Chapter 3, titled 'bringing in trust into global virtual leadership,' merges business ethical reflections on trust in teams with prior VT key findings on GVL, GVTs, and trust. Subchapter 3.1 introduces trust as the critical factor for leading GVTs successfully and elaborates on the normative premise of trust as the key to effective cooperation in GVTs. Thus, subsection 3.1.1 elucidates why trust is essential for successful team interactions. Subsection 3.1.2 introduces the business ethical concept of the (extended) golden rule, and its do no harm dimension as the primary condition for long-term social cooperation. Subsection 3.1.3 introduces the ethical focal point do no (illegitimate) harm as a point of orientation and thus common ground in GVTs for trust.

Moreover, subchapter 3.2 elaborates on the reality of trust in GVTs by summarizing the challenges to trust-building concerning the formation of trust relationships. It will be shown that trust expectations are based on the illegitimacy of harm whose understanding depends on socio-cultural interpretations (3.2.1). Subsequently, it will be shown that the illegitimacy of harm for trust requires an alignment of individual mental models concerning its understanding to create a shared understanding (3.2.2). Finally, in subsection 3.2.3, the importance of GVL to role model trustworthiness will be brought forward. Subchapter 3.3, titled 'Investment in Trust,' represents the quintessence of this dissertation and merges all relevant key findings from previous subsections to answer the research question. Thus, the model of good leadership by Suchanek (2019) is introduced alongside the following four dimensions of trust can be realized: showing respect to GVT members (3.3.1), providing a frame of orientation by creating a shared (team) mental model of illegitimate harm (3.3.2), setting conditions for trust (3.3.3) and acting as a role model through trustworthy behavior while showing consistency in communication and actions (3.3.4). Subchapter 3.4 Case Illustration introduces a real-life case and a tailor-made leadership seminar based on the model of good leadership (Suchanek 2019) for the company Think-It.

Chapter 4 provides the conclusion of this thesis and an outlook for future research and the relevance of the subject matter of GVL, GVTs, and trust.

Understanding Global Virtual Teams and Leadership

2

2.1 Definition of Global Virtual Teams and Leadership

The following section elaborates a working definition of the research object of global virtual teams (GVTs) and global virtual leadership (GVL). GVT research does not offer a comprehensive and agreed-on definition for both terms (Fajen, 2018; Scott & Wildman, 2015). Definitions and demarcation criteria often vary or include partial overlaps in meaning with regard to specific research realms. Additionally, many VT researchers interchange virtual teams (VTs) and virtual leadership (VL) with global or multicultural virtual teams and leadership. This thesis will bring forward various definitions of both terms to give a holistic overview and comprehensive analysis of GVTs and GVL. This thesis will base the following definitions of GVTs and GVL on the findings of Fajen's (2018) comprehensive analyses of multicultural virtual teams and leadership while further complementing these findings with additional input from other researchers deemed necessary for the overall understanding, demarcation, and definition of the objects of research of GVTs and GVL. First, the concept of global will be defined. Second, the idea of VTs will be elaborated. Third, the concept of virtuality and the dimensions of dispersion will be elucidated, and finally, the term leadership will be defined.

2.1.1 Global

In this present thesis, the concept of global encompasses the concepts of *culture*, *diversity*, *socio-cultural distance*, and *multiculturalism*. First, regarding the concept of *culture*, every individual who works in a corporate context is influenced

L. Jassemi, *Global Virtual Teams & Trust*, Gabler Theses,
https://doi.org/10.1007/978-3-658-41852-6_2

by many cultures, including their own national culture and the corporate culture or the culture of a particular department (Fajen, 2018). Even though corporate culture or a department's culture influences employees' actions, this subsection will focus on the definition of national culture. It will do so as the composition of GVTs includes members from at least three different national cultures (Fajen, 2018, p. 25). Thus, this thesis will use national culture and culture as synonyms and will not further refer to this distinction in the following subsections.

An essential part of culture includes patterns that influence thinking, feeling, and acting (Hofstede, 1984, 1993). These are part of a learning process and are mostly developed in the early childhood development phases. Culture is thus a mental program that determines how a person reacts (Hofstede, 1993, p. 18). However, as deviations from the learned thinking, feeling, and acting patterns are possible, culture only predicts the likelihood of specific reactions of people. Culture is not free from external influences; each culture mutually influences the other (Hofstede, 1993). Thus, cultures can further evolve and change through interactions with the social and natural environment, for example, through cultural exchange with people from other national cultures or as a result of specific environmental situations. Culture is reflected in values that guide groups and individuals in their actions or non-actions. It is, therefore, further developed or adapted through people's actions and can thus be understood as a dynamic concept (Hofstede, 1993, 2011).

A collective phenomenon that serves as a demarcation criterion, culture is shared by a certain group. Thus respective cultures differentiate people from others (Hofstede, 1993, p. 19). To compare different cultures with one another, researchers from different disciplines, such as anthropologists, cultural scientists, and sociologists, have developed empirically supported models that describe cultures using cultural dimensions (Fajen, 2018, p. 30). According to prominent intercultural researcher Geert Hofstede, a cultural dimension is an aspect of a culture that can be measured with regard to other cultures (Hofstede, 1993, p. 29). As part of cross-cultural studies, Hofstede's research contains a large empirical basis and replication studies to compare the cultural dimensions of national countries (Hofstede, 1984, 2013).[1] In Hofstede's research, the examined countries are assigned values for each cultural dimension that indicate whether this dimension is strong or weak, allowing for clustering countries into different country groups

---

[1] Further cross-cultural studies providing multidimensional cultural models emanate from Kluckhohn and Stroedbeck (1961), Hall (1966) and Schwartz (1994), and the GLOBE Study by House et al. (2004)

(Hofstede, 1993). This categorization provides relevant explanations for the influence of culture on communication and leadership behavior. This thesis will further refer to this point in the following subsections regarding GVT members' socio-culturally diversity and its impact on cooperation and, more specifically, on trust (2.2.3, 3.2.1, 3.2.2).

Second, further definitions relevant for the comprehensibility of the concept of *global* include the concepts of *diversity* and *socio-cultural distance.* Various dimensions of diversity have been developed to categorize the different characteristics considered under the term diversity (Morrison-Smith & Ruiz, 2020). The most common subdivision of diversity differentiates between observable and non-observable types of diversity summarized in surface-level, deep-level, and functional-level diversity (Milliken & Martins, 1996, p. 404). Surface-level diversity is visible in a team context and refers to ethnic background, age, and sex differences. These characteristics are marked by the fact that they cannot be changed or are difficult to change (Milliken & Martins, 1996). While surface-level diversity reflects primarily observable differences, deep-level diversity consists of less visible differences reflected in personal characteristics such as values, beliefs, and attitudes communicated through extended, personalized interaction and information gathering (Batarseh et al., 2017; Milliken & Martins, 1996). Functional-level diversity refers to the degree to which team members vary in knowledge, information, expertise, and skills (Batarseh et al., 2017, p. 4). GVTs are often more diverse than traditional monocultural or multicultural teams (Fajen, 2018). GVT members often differ in national culture, age, and gender and hold different and complementary roles, often from other departments or company units, in some cases even different companies (Batarseh et al., 2017; Fajen, 2018).

Additionally, diversity is related to and reflected in the *socio-cultural distance,* another concept relevant to the definition of GVTs and GVL. Cultural attitudes, beliefs, values, history, and knowledge systems are interdependent with the social environment, such as community, relationships, and economic status (Agerfalk et al., 2005; Walls, 2013). Thus, socio-cultural distance reflects differences in language, and family structures, for example, in monogamous versus polygamous marriages, religion and belief systems, wealth and lifestyle, as well as values (Triandis & Gelfand, 1998). Within a corporate context, socio-cultural distance has been defined as a measurement of a team member's perception of their teammate's values and usual practices as well as national culture, language, politics, and motivations (Agerfalk et al., 2005). Thus, as GVTs are more socio-culturally diverse than co-located teams, they are marked by higher socio-cultural distance.

Finally, the concept of global further includes the term *multiculturalism.* The term multiculturalism derives from the Latin term "multus," meaning "a lot" or "numerous" (Fajen, 2018). With regards to teams, this means that team members have to belong to at least three or more different national cultures to be referred to as multicultural (Earley & Gibson, 2002) or global in the context of this thesis. Moreover, this thesis shares the following opinion with regards to the object of research of GVTs:

> Multiculturalism is a system of beliefs and behaviors that recognizes and respects the presence of all diverse groups in an organization or society, acknowledges and values their socio-cultural differences, and encourages and enables their continued contribution within an inclusive cultural context which empowers all within the organization or society (Rosado, 1996, p. 2)

Thus, based on the above-elaborated analysis of the consequent concepts of culture, diversity, socio-cultural distance, and multiculturalism, the concept of global defines in this present work a socio-culturally diverse team composed of at least three different national cultures.

2.1.2 Virtual Teams

The concept of virtual teams (VTs) encompasses the definitions of *group, work group, team* as well as *virtuality.* There is a multitude of definitions referring to the term of group. Fajen's (2018) selection of prominent group definitions from sociology, organizational and economic social psychology amongst others serve as guideline for the subsequent analysis of the term group. These include the approaches of Alderfer (1977), Hackman (1987) and Guzzo and Dickson (1996) as main point of reference (Fajen, 2018, p. 35).

According to Alderfer (1977) is a human group a collection of individuals who has significantly interdependent relations with each other. They perceive themselves as a group and are perceived by non-group members as a group and there can be different roles among group members (Alderfer, 1977, p. 230). Moreover, with regards to work groups Hackman (1987) defines these as real groups operating within an organizational context with differentiated roles among members, with one or more tasks to perform, resulting in potentially measurable group products (Hackman, 1987, p. 322). Based on Alderfer (1977) and Hackman (1987) definitions, Guzzo and Dickson (1996) further elaborate that:

> a work group is made up of individuals who see themselves and who are seen by others as a social entity, who are interdependent because of the tasks they perform as members of a group, who are embedded in one or more larger social systems (e.g. community, organization), and who perform tasks that affect others (such as customers or co-workers). (Guzzo & Dickson, 1996, pp. 308–309)

With regards to the number of group members the majority of scientists agree that a group is composed by at least three people (Wahren, 1994). Thus, the term work group refers to a group that consists of at least three people who perceive themselves as a group and who are also perceived as a group from the outside and who work together within a company context to fulfil a common task (Fajen, 2018, p. 37).

Moreover, in organizational psychology and especially in practice the term team is more frequently used than the term work group (Guzzo & Dickson, 1996). While some scientists use both terms synonymously (Earley & Gibson, 2002) others see clear demarcations between the two terms (Wahren, 1994). The more popular opinion is that teams represent more than just work groups (Guzzo & Dickson, 1996). In this regard represents each team a group, but not each group represents a team. Teams are marked by intense mutual relationships with team members being interdependent and consequently working closely together to carry out their tasks (Guzzo & Dickson, 1996, pp. 308–309). Moreover, another characteristic of teams is cohesion which is positively correlated with their interdependency. The more dependent the team members are on each other, the stronger their cohesive behaviour. Moreover, the cohesion in the group is strengthened by common goals which guide work processes (Antoni & Antoni, 2000). Teams are further marked by a division of roles which is necessary to define the functions in the team and the responsibility of the individual members for tasks in order to reduce complexity. A team is thus more than the sum of its members, because it is made up of people whose skills complement each other, creating synergy effects (Antoni & Antoni, 2000; Guzzo & Dickson, 1996).

Thus, in the context of this thesis the concept of team refers to a work group realizing teamwork based on intense cooperation and marked by mutual relationships and cohesion between team members. As part of the cooperation between the team members, rules can be created and roles can be assigned to achieve common goals. The leader of the team is also part of the team (Fajen, 2018, p. 40).

Furthermore, with regards to the definition of VTs there is no clear definition nor consensus among academics. In the predominantly English-language literature on VTs, synonyms for "virtual team" are often used such as the terms of "distributed team", "dispersed team", "computer-mediated team" or "technology-supported team" amongst others (Fajen, 2018; Scott & Wildman, 2015). Moreover, most VT research does not distinguish between VT, GVT or multicultural VT either. Thus, VT researchers agree that it is difficult to summarize and compare research results (Gibson & Gibbs, 2006). In order to proceed with the definition of VT it should be elaborated in what way VTs differ from a traditional or co-located teams. The majority of the authors agree that the members of VTs have to be geographically distributed (Jarvenpaa & Leidner, 1999; T. Kayworth & Leidner, 2000; Maznevski & Chudoba, 2000; Townsend et al., 1998). While members of traditional teams are in close proximity to one another, VT members work in at least two different locations. In extreme cases all members work in different locations. However, there is no consensus in the scientific literature about how to determine the location in a virtual team context. For some researchers, the distribution of team members across different floors of a building is sufficient, as their research results show that even small distances can have an impact on the effectiveness and efficiency of teams (Siebdrat et al., 2009). For others virtual team work starts if its team members are distributed in different buildings, cities and even countries (Maznevski & Chudoba, 2000; O'Leary & Cummings, 2007). This thesis considers the geographical dispersion with regards to different buildings, cities and, countries of team members as defining for the definition of VTs.

Moreover, due to the geographical distribution VTs are marked by reduced or non-existent face-to-face contact, thus they make mostly use of information and communication technology (ICT) for their communication and collaboration (Jarvenpaa & Leidner, 1999; Lipnack & Stamps, 1999; Maznevski & Chudoba, 2000; Townsend et al., 1998). Traditional team members use information and communication media only in addition to face-to-face collaboration.

Thus, based on the given analysis this thesis defines *VTs* as a work group of two or more geographically distributed team members realizing teamwork based on intense cooperation to achieve common goals by using mostly information and communication media. Rules can be created and roles can be distributed in these teams (Fajen, 2018, p. 46).

2.1.3 Virtuality and the Dimensions of Dispersion in Global Virtual Teams

Virtual teams (VTs) can be further deconstructed concerning their degree of virtuality and the dimensions of dispersions of their members. Previous research predominantly focuses on a dichotomous understanding of traditional or co-located teams and VTs. Although they are rarely found in practice, these extreme forms of teams have been the focus of many studies before the beginning of the 21st century (Warkentin et al., 1997). Furthermore, the different degrees of team virtuality, often observed in practice, have also largely been disregarded. The sole measurement of VTs has long been their geographical distribution (Fajen, 2018). This one-dimensional operationalization of team virtuality and the dichotomous comparison of traditional teams and VTs have limited the findings regarding the influence of virtuality on the individual and team level in the past (O'Leary & Cummings, 2007).

Since the beginning of the 21st century, different dimensions of virtuality have been distinguished in VT literature, and indices were developed to calculate them (Jarvenpaa & Leidner, 1999; Lipnack & Stamps, 1999; Maznevski & Chudoba, 2000; Townsend et al., 1998). Virtuality determines whether a team is more or less virtual (Gibson & Gibbs, 2006). Instead of virtuality, some VT researchers also talk about the distribution or dispersion of a team (O'Leary & Cummings, 2007).

This present thesis draws on the most commonly used model by O'Leary and Cummings (2007) for conceptualizing and operationalizing the term team virtuality. Further virtuality factors such as those brought forward by Wilson et al. (2008), Fiol and O'Connor (2005), Gibson and Gibbs (2006), and Kirkman and Mathieu (2005) will be introduced too. O'Leary and Cummings (2007) concepts measure the degree of the virtuality of teams regarding three types of distribution or dispersion, namely spatial, time and structure. The spatial distribution is based on the physical distance in km between team members, whereas the temporal distribution refers to the time zones over which team members are distributed (O'Leary & Cummings, 2007). The structural distribution is based on the number of team locations and on the number of team members who work in isolation, i.e., alone at their location, and on how the team members are distributed across the locations, i.e., even, or uneven distribution of team members, in different locations.

Moreover, spatial and temporal dispersion is commonly conceptualized as a distance factor (Morrison-Smith & Ruiz, 2020). Another distance factor growing in prominence in VT research is perceived distance or perceived proximity (Wilson et al., 2008). Perceived distance is characterized by a person's impression of how near or how far another person is and is, therefore, a matter of subjectivity. It has an affective and a cognitive component (O'Leary et al., 2012). Perceived distance is thus very distinct from a spatial-temporal distance and even not necessarily related (Morrison-Smith & Ruiz, 2020). Instead, perceived distance is the symbolic meaning of proximity having a more significant effect on relationship outcomes (O'Leary et al., 2012).

Moreover, Gibson and Gibbs (2006) combine four dimensions to discern the virtuality level: geographical dispersion, electronic dependence, dynamic structure, and national diversity (Jawadi, 2013, p. 22). Other commonly used distribution factors refer to the degree of face-to-face contact (Fiol & O'Connor, 2005). Other authors focus on technological dimensions such as the use of virtual tools to coordinate and execute team processes, the amount of informational value provided by such tools, and the synchronicity of team member virtual interaction (Kirkman & Mathieu, 2005).

Overall, most VT researchers nowadays agree that the dimensions of dispersion or virtuality are a combination of different factors mentioned above and thus a composite construct that indicates the degree of virtuality in the team, reflecting how technology helps or impedes its performance (Hacker et al., 2019; Morrison-Smith & Ruiz, 2020). VT researchers place teams thus on a continuum from entirely virtual to face-to-face (Fiol & O'Connor, 2005; Ford et al., 2017).

2.1.4 Leadership of Global Virtual Teams

In this thesis, the *leadership* of global virtual teams (GVTs) is defined as global virtual leadership (GVL). The definition of GVL is based on examining traditional leadership research, including management sciences and organizational psychology regarding GVTs. Further reflections from leadership ethics (chapter 3) will be added concerning successful GVL.

First, the concept of leadership must be distinguished from the closely related concept of management before proceeding to give an overall working definition of GVL. Management can be defined as goal-oriented and steered action (Jung et al., 2011). As part of the functional management approach, this definition focuses on the various tasks and functions and their coordination in a company (Fajen, 2018). The main tasks of management relate thus to planning, organizing, and control within all corporate realms like, for example, production, procurement, and accounting realized by the manager.

Regarding leadership, the most relevant literature refers leading employees or people in general (Jung et al., 2011). This conceptual understanding of leadership is shared in this present work. Moreover, the leadership of people is also connected with planning, organizational, and control tasks. Still, unlike management, these are not related to the overall corporate level but to individual people or teams (Fajen, 2018, p. 132). Earlier leadership approaches postulate that the direction of action of leadership emanates from the superior down. However, most researchers agree that leadership is a dynamic process of mutual influence based on interactions (Hollander, 1978). According to Hollander (1978) is, "leadership a process of influence between a leader and those who are followers" (p. 1). In this regard, leaders and employees mutually influence each other, for example, through feedback loops and communication exchange (Northouse, 2013). However, the leader initiates the communication processes while building and maintaining relationships with employees. Furthermore, there are different levels of leadership. In addition to leading individual people, referred to in the literature as dyadic leadership, there is also the leadership of groups or teams (Northouse, 2013).

The subsequent analysis of the terms global (cf. 2.1.1), VTs (cf. 2.1.2), virtuality, and dimensions of dispersion (cf. 2.1.3) and leadership conclude with a definition of the object of research of GVTs and GVL.

Thus, GVTs are defined as socio-culturally diverse work teams with intense interdependent relationships with members from at least three different national cultures. Further, GVTs are marked by spatial, temporal, and structural dispersion. Their members work in at least two different geographical locations while relying on information and communication technology to realize shared goals. Rules can be created in GVTs, and roles can be assigned to different members.

Building on this definition of GVTs, GVL refers to personnel leadership and is understood as a process of targeted influence of one or more global virtual team members. Global virtual leaders are, in this context, the people entrusted with the leadership of GVTs.

2.2 Global Virtual Teams in Practice

This subsection gives insights about global virtual teams (GVTs) in practice. First, it will shed light on the rise of GVTs and the benefits of their employment (2.2.1). Second, it will summarize the challenges of GVTs regarding communication, the use of technology, and socio-cultural differences under the umbrella of communication effectiveness (2.2.2). Finally, it will show how these communication effectiveness challenges impact cooperation and performance in GVTs (2.2.3).

2.2.1 The Rise and Benefits of Global Virtual Teams

Since the 1970 s, several trends have pathed the rise of virtual work related to the history of telecommuting, the story of information transfer, and technological development (Weiler Reynolds & Bibby, 2017). The Clean Air Act (1970), the OPEC oil embargo (1973), and the awful commuter traffic into and out of cities have seen the telecommuting workplace emerging (Pasini, 2018). To offset traffic congestion and conserve resources, Jack Nilles' model of flexible work arrangement (FWA), as described in his book 'The Telecommunications-Transportation Tradeoff '(1973), caught on quickly in policy and industry alike (Weiler Reynolds & Bibby, 2017). Thus, in 1978, the U.S. government passed the first FWA policy, granting flexible schedules to federal employees. This trend further spread to industries with telecommunication advancements that made working from various locations possible (Weiler Reynolds & Bibby, 2017). American companies like J.C. Penney or American Express started hiring home-based call center agents to cut costs and offer employment incentives and thus inspired other companies worldwide to follow (Pasini, 2018).

Moreover, the launch of the Windows operating system in 1985 revolutionized personal and business computing by incorporating computers into daily employee tasks (Pasini, 2018). In 1991, the World Wide Web browser was released to the public, offering individuals access to networks of data and information-sharing capabilities, further allowing professionals from home options. In 1998 Google was founded and rapidly grew into the Internet's leading search engine, further accelerating virtual work's rise (Pasini, 2018). Since the 2000 s, technological development and new communication tools, as well as the emergence of social media, third generation (3G) mobile devices, and streaming technology, have further established home working options (Pasini, 2018). The introduction of broadband service for mobile phones in 2001 enhanced data transfer capacities, with more devices connected to the Internet. New handled devices like Apple's iPhone release in 2007 changed how individuals accessed and used information (Pasini, 2018).

Moreover, software applications like Slack, Hootsuite, Skype, or lately Zoom have emerged and enabled employees to collaborate and work from remote locations. Advancements in cloud computing also made remote teamwork more effective and accessible. Additionally, co-working and living spaces have emerged and offer individuals and start-ups alternative work environments (Pasini, 2018).

These communication trends, enhanced methods of information transfer, and technological developments have been accompanied and enabled by the overall trend of economic activity of all types moving in the direction of globalization

(Acs & Preston, 1997). The growing popularity of inter-organizational alliances and a growing tendency to flatter organizational structures have accelerated the need for firms to coordinate geographically dispersed activities (Townsend et al., 1998). In addition, the shift from production to service-related businesses has spawned a new generation of knowledge workers not bound to physical work locations (Kayworth & Leidner, 2000, p. 183).

Furthermore, virtual, or remote work has seen a massive push due to the unprecedented outbreak of the COVID-19 global pandemic in 2020. Millions of employees worldwide have been forced into remote work, with broad implications for organizations and employees (Kniffin et al., 2021). Remote work was not widespread before the global pandemic, although it grew steadily (Kossek & Lautsch, 2018). According to the American Community Survey (2017), the number of U.S. employees who worked from home at least half the time grew from 1.8 million in 2005 to 3.9 million in 2017. Remote working only comprised 2.9 percent of the U.S. workforce (Wang et al., 2021, p. 17). In Europe, only 2 percent of employees were remote workers in 2015 (Eurofound, 2017). Until now, remote working has been mostly practiced and offered to higher-income earners (e.g., over 75% of employees who work from home have an annual earning above $65,000) and white-collar workers (e.g., over 40% of teleworkers are executives, managers, or professionals) (Wang et al., 2021, p. 17). Thus, before the global pandemic, most employees had little to no remote working experience, nor were they or their organizations prepared to support this practice on a large scale.

During the early part of the global pandemic, 80% of global corporate work policies have shifted to virtual and mixed forms of virtual team collaboration (Meluso et al., 2020). Furthermore, regarding CMC, new apps like Zoom have become integral to remote working practices. Thus, many organizations are planning a unique combination of remote and on-site work, giving rise to a hybrid work model (Wang et al., 2021, p. 17). Even before the global pandemic, virtual work was increasing in all kinds of organizations, with new collaborative software, video conferencing, and online project management software being released regularly for the global marketplace. Thus, virtual work is one of the biggest drivers of the transformation in the workplace (Powers, 2018, p. 7).

Especially GVTs and their socio-culturally diverse workforce are growing in prevalence as they maintain the increasingly globalized social and economic infrastructure (Morrison-Smith & Ruiz, 2020, p. 1). GVTs can positively impact people and the planet if these teams are designed to embrace technology and prioritize communication and relationships with a strong appreciation of culture and diversity (Powers, 2018). There are various strategic benefits of employing GVTs as they combine the advantages of culturally diverse and VTs. Based on previous VT research, numerous chances arise for companies and employees alike (Bergiel et al., 2008; Cascio, 2000; Hertel et al., 2005; T. Kayworth & Leidner, 2000; Maznevski & Chudoba, 2000).

First, most VT authors agree that the main advantage of employing GVTs is the possibility to recruit talents worldwide to use their expertise regardless of their location and nationality (Bergiel et al., 2008; Kayworth & Leidner, 2000, p. 183). Moreover, GVTs are entrusted with a wide variety of tasks that are often complex and of great strategic importance for companies, such as developing new products or realizing global marketing activities (Cascio, 2000). Through global virtual teamwork, the know-how of globally distributed experts can be utilized (Maznevski & Chudoba, 2000). The automotive industry is a prominent field of employment for GVTs. Team members depend highly on each other for their tasks, which require diverse competencies from various areas and country-specific information (Bergiel et al., 2008). GVTs are particularly suitable for knowledge-based activities that need to be carried out by experts, as well as for service-intensive activities where employees are in direct contact with customers and should be available around the clock (Townsend et al., 1998). Many European and American companies use foreign companies for their services and development of their products, like the company of the illustration case called Think-it (Think-it, 2022). Think-it is one of these service providers offering software solutions to renowned European and American organizations thanks to their globally dispersed members.

Moreover, companies may save costs due to lower wages in other countries and reduced travel costs for their staff (Kayworth & Leidner, 2000). The employment of GVTs further allows for reducing a company's carbon footprint, which has become more important due to the urgency of taking action to reduce the negative impact of climate change in recent years (Johnson et al., 2001).

In addition, due to the different time zones, projects can be worked on a 24/7 basis (O'Leary & Cummings, 2007). According to the 'follow the sun' approach, which allows work to be accomplished on an ongoing basis shifting from one time zone to another, companies can gain a significant competitive advantage (Treinen & Miller-Frost, 2006). They can not only offer their services almost unlimitedly but improve them thanks to continuous, direct contact with customers (Cascio, 2000).

Besides, the multicultural and diverse nature of GVTs allows companies to respond to the needs of multicultural stakeholders and gives them access to global markets (Cascio, 2000, p. 82). The diverse cultural background of the team members allows for a better understanding of the local political, social, and economic conditions in the country markets relevant to the company (Kayworth & Leidner, 2000). In addition, the socio-cultural diversity of GVTs offers a variety of perspectives, which is reflected in enhanced creativity and flexibility in the thinking and acting of employees and leaders alike as well as a multitude of different problem-solving approaches (Fajen, 2018). While there are many challenges associated with the multiculturalism present in culturally diverse GVTs, multiculturalism is an enrichment for the whole team, especially for the leader: "[T]o be an effective manager […] you always have to be learning, and I look at my employees from different cultures as tremendous resources to me and my learning." (Fajen, 2018, p. 81).

With regards to GVT members, there are a variety of benefits of virtual work. Virtual collaboration allows, for example, an improvement of psycho-social aspects in the team (Cascio, 2000). Compared to traditional co-located teams, virtual work provides a better work-life balance and thus reduces the stress of employees related to traveling. Furthermore, due to the geographical and spatial flexibility, work processes can be adapted to the individual preferences of team members, improving employee contentment and commitment (Cascio, 2000). These possibilities of choice and freedom in virtual work organizations make them generally more attractive for employees (Kayworth & Leidner, 2000). According to a recent study by GitLab with 3000 diverse employees worldwide, virtual work is highly in demand. Many employees are considering resigning from a co-located organization to a company that offers remote work (GitLab, 2020).

Furthermore, there are some advantages to using commuter-mediated communication (CMC) technology in GVTs, like higher decision quality, depth of analysis, equality of participation, and satisfaction (Fjermestad, 2004). Through asynchronous media like emails or texting, team members can take their time when asking a question or crafting a response (Walsh & Maloney, 2007). Thus, time-independent interaction allows a high degree of flexibility (Fajen, 2018). Moreover, asynchronous media provides efficient and focused conversations quicker than other forms of communication (Kraut et al., 2002). CMC use also allows increased participation among team members and facilitates the emergence of unique ideas. Additionally, digital communication reduces the distance between members of different hierarchical statuses and therefore promotes more equality, i.e., concerning the respective shares of speech compared to face-to-face communication (Dubrovsky et al., 1991; Gibson et al., 2014).

Moreover, social differences play a lesser role, and the fear of being directly judged by others is mitigated by the apparent anonymity of CMC (Dubrovsky et al., 1991). Moreover, ethnicity and gender are less visible factors, and discrimination is less likely to occur, promoting more equal opportunities within the team (Bergiel et al., 2008). CMC's anonymity also makes it easier for team members to discuss sensitive issues more openly. Regarding conflicts, asynchronous communication media offers a specific type of protection as individual team members have the opportunity to reflect on their positions and prepare for discussions, which is particularly helpful if they do not share the same native language (Hertel et al., 2008).

In sum, global virtual work can offer organizations and employees various benefits and advantages. More specifically, the employment of GVTs provides a significant opportunity to coordinate complex business tasks across a potentially far-flung confederation of organizations (Kayworth & Leidner, 2000, p. 184). Thus, organizations increasingly rely on GVTs (Morrison-Smith & Ruiz, 2020). However, the rise of virtual work has impacted how people connect, how teams communicate, how leaders build relationships, and how organizations fulfill their tasks and accomplish their results (Powers, 2018, pp. 6–7). These factors suggest that organizations are equally faced with increased challenges to coordinate tasks across time zones, physical boundaries, and cultures, including leadership for effective collaboration and performance of GVTs (Kayworth & Leidner, 2000, p. 183). The following subchapter will elucidate the challenges that GVTs face concerning communication, the use of technology, and socio-cultural differences (2.2.2).

2.2.2 Challenges Related to Communication, the Use of Technology and Socio-Cultural Distance in Global Virtual Teams

Many studies have examined the challenges of employing global virtual teams (GVTs), especially concerning their efficient collaboration and performance. First, this subsection will overview some of the main authors' key findings regarding the overall challenges and factors that impact collaboration and performance in GVTs. Second, all relevant challenges will be summarized with regrad to communication, the use of technology, and socio-cultural distance. These challenges overall resume in communication effectiveness challenges impacting team cooperation and performance in GVTs.

First, prominent VT in-depth research by Olson and Olson (2000, 2006) has analyzed the challenges of employing GVTs. Based on more than ten years of laboratory and field research examining synchronous collaboration of remote and co-located workers, Olson and Olson have identified ten challenges that hinder distance work summarized in challenges with regards to 1) awareness of colleagues and their context, 2) motivational sense of the presence of others, 3) trust, 4) the level of technical competence of team members, 5) the level of technical infrastructure, 6) nature of work, 7) explicit management, 8) common ground, 9) competitive corporative culture, and 10) alignment of incentives and goals.

Further research on specifically global virtual teams (GVTs) by Kayworth and Leidner (2000, 2002) in a field-based study assessed the core issues and challenges faced by a group of twelve culturally diverse GVT members from Europe, Mexico, and the United States. Their research findings suggest that GVT faces significant challenges in the areas of 1) communication, 2) culture, 4) technology, and 5) project management (leadership). Based on the members' assessments of their virtual team experiences, each challenge area is discussed in detail and offers a set of managerial prescriptions that outline critical success factors useful for implementing GVTs.

Moreover, Smith and Ruiz (2020) have put together an extensive literature review to highlight the collaboration challenges experienced by VTs in general and with particular regard to their use of technology while offering mitigation strategies. Based on their comprehensive research of a total of 255 relevant studies, including the in-depth analysis of Olson and Olson (2000, 2006) as well as Kayworth and Leidner's research (2000, 2002), they have separated general challenges in VTs as belonging to five distance factor categories with regards to 1) geographical distance, 2) temporal distance, 3) perceived distance and the 4) configuration of dispersed teams and 5) diversity of workers. All distance factors include associated challenges that intersect and impede the overall efficiency of VTs. These factors are coupled with social and emotional factors, including motivation, conflicts, and trust.

In summary, based on the analysis of previous VT research as summarized by the above-given authors, this thesis outlines the challenges of GVTs concerning cooperation and performance under the umbrella of communication, the use of technology, and socio-cultural distance. These factors can be resumed as overall communication effectiveness challenges. This thesis will focus on these challenges as they are relevant for the research topic of this present work regarding their impact on the building of trust in GVTs and the role of GVL in building trust in GVTs.

With regards to overall communication in VTs, previous research agrees that the lack of informal and face-to-face communication in VTs results in a variety of diverse communication challenges impacting performance (Jarvenpaa & Leidner, 1999; T. Kayworth & Leidner, 2000; Olson & Olson, 2000; Olson &

Olson, 2011). The fundamental challenge in VTs is thus associated with effective team communication. Effective communication is essential to group functioning regardless of the environment (e.g., traditional or virtual teams) (Trevino et al., 1990). Communication effectiveness among VTs is impacted by various technical, cultural, and human factors, which are all related and intertwined (Kayworth & Leidner, 2000). The organizational structure, levels of interdependence, and media richness, which range from face-to-face communication to documents, further influence communication effectiveness (Klitmøller & Lauring, 2013).[2]

More specifically, there are several significant challenges related to communication and the use of technology within VTs (Olson & Olson, 2000). In the (near) absence of face-to-face interaction, VTs and their leaders have increased online activity. They rely heavily on various information technologies to communicate among themselves (Kayworth & Leidner, 2000, p. 186). The challenges refer to the impact of CMC technology on communication between team members, leaders, and clients, including the choice of technology for communication, the technical competency of team members and leaders, and the level of technical infrastructure (Morrison-Smith & Ruiz, 2020). This CMC technology includes asynchronous communication like email or text-based tools and synchronous communication like audiovisual and audio. Both are used to transmit, receive and process information, plan and coordinate tasks, take decisions, and exercise control in VTs (Olson & Olson, 2000). Moreover, VTs have to interact, share meaning, and reach consensus in the absence of rich face-to-face interaction but through the use of these CMC.

The choice of CMC technology significantly influences communication because each method offers a different capacity to convey verbal and nonverbal cues (Montoya et al., 2009, p. 142; Morrison-Smith & Ruiz, 2020). The transmission of non-verbal gestures (i.e., gestures, facial expressions, body language) and para-verbal communication elements (i.e., tone of voice, loudness), which are signals that influence the information exchange is limited due to the filtering effect of less rich information and communication media (Bergiel et al., 2008). The resulting problem is that rich social, emotional, and non-verbal information present in traditional face-to-face settings cannot be transferred (Kayworth & Leidner, 2000, p. 187).

Moreover, while CMC is missing important social information, they also take more time and effort to effectively communicate information, further hampering

[2] These factors vary depending on the communication method's capacity for immediate feedback, ability to facilitate non-verbal cues, and level of personalization (Klitmøller & Lauring, 2013).

the establishment of ties between team members (Dubé & Robey, 2009, p. 18). While a physical gesture like a brief nod in face-to-face contexts is sufficient to signal that a message has been received and understood, CMC often requires time-consuming feedback processes such as writing an e-mail to complete the communication process (Dubé & Robey, 2009). This is particularly challenging as most communication in VTs is asynchronous and in written form through emails and texting. It is thus more challenging to determine whether the information within the written communication email was understood due to the absence of vocal and nonverbal cues (Marlow et al., 2017). Additionally, communication effectiveness is hindered due to distortions and unclear messages (Nydegger & Nydegger, 2010, p. 79).

Thus, coordination delays due to the need for clarification of information regularly occur in GVTs and impact team performance negatively, which will be further discussed in detail in 2.2.3. Moreover, additional factors, such as experience with a task, interdependence, and the temporal stage of team development, can impact team performance when relying on CMC technology (Dennis et al., 2008; Marlow et al., 2017). The more teams have experience with the task at hand and with each other the less there is the need for synchronous CMC technology for extra clarification (e.g., video conferencing) (Dennis et al., 2008, pp. 590–591). In contrast, when teams do not have this extensive experience, there is a greater need for synchronous CMC. Therefore the stage at which a virtual team develops affects their communication (Maruping & Agarwal, 2004, p. 978).

Furthermore, the level of technical infrastructure can also create collaboration challenges (Olson & Olson, 2011). For virtual work to function correctly, adequate technical support or resources should be offered. Reliability is also an issue of communication technology. Technology must be stable enough to compete with the well-established reliability of the telephone (Bjørn et al., 2014, p. 18). It comes with that that the level of technical competence of the team members and leader can pose an additional challenge to VTs' performance (Olson & Olson, 2011, p. 1). Teams unable to adopt and integrate basic technology into their everyday workflow are unlikely to use more sophisticated CMC that may better support visual and verbal cues, thus enriching virtual communication (Morrison-Smith & Ruiz, 2020; Olson & Olson, 2000).

Additionally, another challenge concerning communication relates to the high temporal distance between team members of GVTs (Morrison-Smith & Ruiz, 2020, pp. 10–11). Due to high temporal distance, there is a reduced number of overlapping work hours between GVT members (Battin et al., 2001). Thus, it is very challenging to schedule global meetings (Treinen & Miller-Frost, 2006, pp. 777–778).[3] The temporal distance can lead to incompatible schedules that result in project delays and can only be overcome through thorough planning (Cummings, 2011, pp. 25–26). Fewer overlapping work hours result in communication breakdowns, such as an increased need for rework and clarifications and difficulties adjusting to new problems (Espinosa & Carmel, 2004, p. 7; Espinosa & Pickering, 2006, pp. 4–6). As synchronous communication is limited in GVTs, important feedback is often delayed, thus further delaying projects and team results (Agerfalk et al., 2005, p. 7).

Moreover, contributing factors that further impact communication effectiveness in GVTs relate to their configuration (O'Leary & Mortensen, 2010, p. 115). Configuration in GVTs can be divided into site, imbalance, and isolation. While site dispersion is best characterized as the degree to which collaborators are at distinct geographic locations, imbalance refers to the proportion of collaborators dispersed across a set of sites (O'Leary & Cummings, 2007, p. 434). Isolation means that GVT members are on their own at one site. The communication within and between different sites and imbalanced teams or isolated members is very different and hinders effective communication in the overall team. Members at the same sites can communicate face-to-face in addition to using CMC while using CMC for communication with the dispersed team located at different sites. This can distort messages between the whole team and lead to miscommunication while instilling feelings of isolation and alienation (O'Leary & Cummings, 2007; O'Leary & Mortensen, 2010).

Furthermore, socio-cultural distance factors (cf. 2.1.1) profoundly impact communication effectiveness and collaboration in GVTs. Although socio-cultural differences may bring a greater variety of perspectives to bear on a problem domain, they may also create additional communication challenges for team members. Cultural backgrounds impact how individuals perceive information, act upon it, and relate to others (Hofstede, 1984). Individuals filter information through their cultural 'lenses' and socio-cultural perspectives, giving rise to a potentially broad range of misinterpretations or distortions (Hofstede, 1984). The norms, values, and basic assumptions of each individual's culture influence the coding and decoding processes and the type of feedback the communicator gives (Hofstede, 2011). This is particularly relevant in teamwork. While Germans, for example, are known for their directness, many Asians practice a very indirect way of communicating, in which non-verbal communication elements such as facial

[3] It is important to note that initiating spontaneous communication by using the telephone could be perceived as intrusive and inadequate.

expressions and gestures play a predominant role. These differences in communication behavior between people with different socio-cultural backgrounds are characterized by a high degree of complexity and can lead to ambiguity, confusion, miscommunication, and misunderstanding (Holmstrom et al., 2006).

Besides, concerning language, further communication challenges arise if the team language and the native language of all virtual team members are not identical (Holmstrom et al., 2006). Deficits in foreign language competence, culturally influenced connotations, strong accents, or small differences in the choice of words can represent language barriers and lead to further misunderstandings when encoding or decoding virtually transmitted messages (Holmstrom et al., 2006). While in face-to-face communication, the transmission of non-verbal and para-verbal communication elements can counteract these comprehension problems, virtual communication cannot convey subtleties in language through, for example, gestures and facial expressions (Fajen, 2018).

The work culture also reflects the socio-cultural difference (Morrison-Smith & Ruiz, 2020, p. 19). Work culture is reflected in peoples' processes, knowledge, expectations, goals, and conflict resolution mechanisms (Cundill, Harvey, Tebboth, Cochrane, Currie-Alder, et al., 2019). Differences in work culture bear great potential for misunderstandings and even lead to communication breakdowns in GVTs, thus negatively impacting team performance (Agerfalk et al., 2005). GVT members come from various professional backgrounds and have different expertise and experiences, which can create incompatible views on how to work and accomplish tasks and goals (Morrison-Smith & Ruiz, 2020). Additionally, it is very difficult to properly communicate subtle aspects of the team culture over a distance (Armstrong & Cole, 1995).[4]

In sum, due to the lack of informal and face-to-face communication and the heavy use of CMC superseded by socio-cultural differences, various challenges arise in GVTs regarding communication efficiency. The following subsection will give more details about the consequences and impact of these communication effectiveness challenges on cooperation and performance in GVTs.

[4] Different organizations may have diverse work cultures as manifested by deeply held core beliefs and assumptions. Consequently, although individuals may have similar national or ethnic backgrounds, they may still exhibit radically different cultural assumptions as engendered by the organization for whom they work (Kayworth & Leidner, 2000, p. 188).

2.2.3 The Impact of Communication Effectiveness Challenges on Cooperation and Performance in Global Virtual Teams

The previous subsection has shown that the lack of informal and face-to-face communication and the heavy use of communication technologies superseded by socio-cultural differences bear various challenges with regards to communication efficiency in GVTs (cf. 2.2.2). This subsection will further elucidate in detail in what way these challenges impact cooperation and performance in GVTs.

Informal communication and face-to-face encounters play an essential role in collaboration and have been defined by various VT authors as crucial for the effectiveness of teamwork, especially at the beginning of a project in GVTs (Armstrong & Cole, 1995; Dubé & Robey, 2009; Fajen, 2018). Equally important for all kinds of teams, informal communication and face-to-face encounters promote the sense of belonging to the team and the awareness of group activities (Dourish & Bellotti, 1992). Awareness can be understood as an understanding of the activities of others that provides a context for somebody's own activities. This team awareness is important for individual and team performance as it allows to not only stay aware of the developments of others but encourages team members to deliver on their tasks to accomplish the overall team goal (Olson & Olson, 2011). Regarding GVTs, being aware of colleagues and their context is a significant challenge to collaboration due to the distribution of team members (Armstrong & Cole, 1995). Thus, in GVTs, this lack of awareness resumes in team members tending to rely more on potentially biased perceptions and assumptions that can negatively impact collaboration (Peñarroja et al., 2013). Team members are also more disengaged from each other. Collaborative work is, however, significantly delayed without such awareness (Olson & Olson, 2006). Coordination delays decrease performance as they complicate meeting key requirements, staying within the budget, and completing work on time (Olson & Olson, 2011, p. 1).

Additionally, collaborators' delayed responses often occur in GVTs, which is not only annoying for the whole GVT but a time-consuming process, especially concerning solving urgent issues (Holmstrom et al., 2006). For example, suppose a specific team member is unavailable when their expertise is needed. In that case, it can lead other GVT members to resolve the issue by making assumptions based on local culture and preferences and cause additional rework if the outcome is wrong (Agerfalk et al., 2005). Moreover, coordination delays increase the spatial-temporal distance between GVT members, thus further negatively impacting GVT performance (Cummings, 2011).

Furthermore, the heavy use of CMC is a time-consuming process and equally takes more effort to effectively communicate (Dubé & Robey, 2009; Marlow et al., 2017). GVT members need to use CMC intensely to convey information for effective communication and cooperation and are thus required to manage high volumes of messages (Marlow et al., 2017). Moreover, in GVT, members may also divide their attention between various tasks while simultaneously participating in teamwork interactions, thus resulting in a lack of investment in these tasks (Marlow et al., 2017; Morrison-Smith & Ruiz, 2020). This can further complicate GVT cooperation and thus decrease performance primarily when team members work closely interdependently on projects.

Also, these communication effectiveness problems can negatively impact GVT decision-making processes (McNamara et al., 2008). Through CMC technology, failures to integrate important information can occur; thus, key elements for the decision situation are omitted, impairing performance (McNamara et al., 2008, p. 29). Additionally, some members may be excluded from spontaneous decisions that are made outside formal virtual meetings, for example, among those who live in close proximity and have the potential for face-to-face encounters.

Moreover, this lack of face-to-face contact and informal communication results in GVTs having a lower sense of cohesion and personal relationships with their team members (Warkentin et al., 1997). Informal communication, which often occurs after meetings or during unexpected encounters in the hallway leading to coffee talk, are possibilities to not only share knowledge for team and task awareness but to build personal rapports which support the building of trust (Agerfalk et al., 2005). However, in GVTs, these possibilities are less given; thus, formal and informal information will be less shared, making it more difficult to maintain social contacts with team members. Furthermore, crucial social information essential to building bonds between team members is more difficult to transmit through CMC (Dubé & Robey, 2009). Overall, GVT members may have a less affective commitment to their team, negatively affecting team cooperation and performance (Johnson et al., 2009).

Additionally, contributing factors that further impact communication effectiveness in GVTs relate to their configuration (O'Leary & Mortensen, 2010, p. 115). Configuration in GVTs can be divided into site, imbalance, and isolation. While site dispersion is best characterized as the degree to which collaborators are at distinct geographic locations, imbalance refers to the proportion of collaborators dispersed across a set of sites (O'Leary & Cummings, 2007, p. 434). Isolation means that GVT members are on their own at one site. All three configuration dispersions can impact GVT collaboration negatively. They can create, for instance, fault lines that escalate polarization, subgrouping, and the effect of causing collaborators in other locations to feel more distant (Durnell Cramton & Hinds, 2004).

Besides, the challenges related to communication effectiveness in GVTs can create conflicts and feelings of isolation, further adding to cooperation and performance issues (Morrison-Smith & Ruiz, 2020). Conflicts frequently occur in GVTs due to biases, assumptions, and miscommunication (Herbsleb et al., 2000). Like in traditional teams, GVTs experience affective (i.e., interpersonal), task-based, or process-based conflicts (i.e., related to responsibilities and tasks) (Jehn, 1997). However, some GVT researchers have concluded that GVTs experience higher levels of conflict (Armstrong & Cole, 1995; Herbsleb et al., 2000; Hinds & Mortensen, 2005; O'Leary & Mortensen, 2010). GVTs are particularly prone to interpersonal and task-based conflicts, which can be even more detrimental than traditional teams (Mortensen & Hinds, 2001). This is because disagreements in distributed teams can potentially escalate into full-blown conflicts more efficiently while remaining unresolved for extended periods (Armstrong & Cole, 1995). More specifically, GVTs often experience intra-team conflicts (Armstrong & Cole, 1995) as part of interpersonal conflicts (Jehn, 1997). Intra-team conflicts result from site dispersion and imbalanced teams leading to subgrouping of team members. Subgrouping can lead to limited information flow within the team, reducing team cohesion and false and harsh attributions between team members (Cramton, 2001). Intra-team conflicts provoke an us-versus-them attitude between dispersed team members at different sites (Armstrong & Cole, 1995; Cramton, 2001). Thus, intra-team conflicts often result in project delays, further undermining team effectivity (Armstrong & Cole, 1995; Herbsleb et al., 2000).

Moreover, high site dispersion is associated with higher amounts of fault lines (Durnell Cramton & Hinds, 2004).Specifically, fault lines escalate polarization and cause team members that do not work at more significant sites with more members to feel alienated from the whole team. Moreover, high site dispersion further accentuates socio-cultural differences, which can underpin these divisions (Durnell Cramton & Hinds, 2004). Thus, high site dispersion is associated with decreased knowledge sharing, delays in work processes, less team performance (Gibson & Gibbs, 2006), and project failure (Cummings & Kiesler, 2005).

Overall, the challenges of communication effectiveness in GVTs resulting from the lack of informal and face-to-face communication, the heavy use of communication technologies superseded by socio-cultural differences can lead to a variety of cooperation and performance issues in GVTs and should thus not be underestimated by GVL.

The following section 2.3 will elaborate on the challenges that GVL faces in overcoming the communication effectiveness challenges in GVTs (cf. 2.2.2) and their impact on cooperation and performance (cf. 2.2.3) and offers insights into mitigation strategies elaborated by previous GVT research (2.3.1). Moreover, it will be shown that specific leadership competencies and roles successful GVL should fulfill (2.3.2). More importantly, regarding the research object of GVTs, GVL, and trust, subsection 2.3.3 will elaborate on why trust is a fundamental condition for leading effective GVTs for cooperation and performance.

2.3 Global Virtual Leadership

As organizations seek to leverage the potential benefits of global virtual teams (GVTs), they must face the numerous complexities inherent in this new organizational structure. According to prior GVT research, the leadership of GVTs represents the most significant challenge (Fajen, 2018; Kayworth & Leidner, 2000). As previous research has pointed out, the main problem in virtual organizational settings is related to the lack of physical interaction and the absence or near absence of non-verbal cues resulting in a variety of challenges related to communication, the use of technology, and socio-cultural differences (cf. 2.2.2) that negatively impact cooperation and performance in GVT (cf. 2.2.3). Thus, GVL's task is to overcome these challenges in GVTs for effective cooperation and performance and find ways to bridge the spatial, temporal and structural dispersion in GVTs. This subsection will elucidate this point further. First, it will lay out the general challenges and tasks of GVL (2.3.1). Second, it will be shown that a successful GVL needs specific leadership competencies and has to fulfill a variety of so-called e-roles[5] (2.3.2). Finally, this section will elucidate why building trust in GVTs is one of the main conditions for effective cooperation and performance and thus an essential task for successful GVL (2.3.3).

2.3.1 Leadership Challenges and Mitigation Strategies

Like leaders of traditional teams, the tasks of global virtual leaders include developing strategies for the team and assigning tasks and roles according to the

[5] E stands for electronic. Fajen (2018) describes twelve e-roles for successful GVL based on her extensive research on multicultural virtual leadership. These roles will be summarized in 2.3.2.

qualifications of team members (Zaccaro & Bader, 2003). GVL's duties include ensuring that team members across different locations have all the necessary resources to realize their tasks. GVL has to create common goals, coordinate joint team activities, promote the building of social relationships in the team, and control team results (Fajen, 2018; Zaccaro & Bader, 2003). Even though similar to traditional leadership, the realization of these tasks is more difficult in a global and virtual organizational context. Additionally, while leaders of traditional teams often have to worry about detailed planning due to the physical proximity of their team members, global virtual leaders should not micromanage but have a view of the whole instead, i.e., to observe and coordinate the team's overall activities and enable team cohesion for effective cooperation (Fajen, 2018, p. 328). Moreover, due to the high degree of socio-cultural diversity of GVTs, resulting in different ways of thinking and acting and consequently harboring the potential for disagreements, GVL is required to accommodate the needs of all parties and establish consensus while defusing potential conflicts (Fajen, 2018).

Thus, successful GVL is required to fulfill all the tasks mentioned above while overcoming the overall challenges inherent to GVTs related to spatial, temporal, and structural dispersion (Fajen, 2018; Warkentin et al., 1997; Zaccaro & Bader, 2003).

Moreover, according to prior VT research, the most significant challenge and most important task for successful GVL represents the building of mutual trust (Fajen, 2018; Hunsaker & Hunsaker, 2008; Jarvenpaa & Leidner, 1999; Lipnack & Stamps, 1999; Zaccaro & Bader, 2003). Due to the absence of nonverbal cues and the inability to infer the nature of others' intentions, relationship building and especially the building of interpersonal trust may be hampered (Zigurs, 2003, p. 344).[6] Thus, previous VT research agrees that compared to the leadership of traditional teams, the leadership of GVTs, especially the building of trust, is more complicated, complex, and time-consuming (Fajen, 2018, p. 270). Thus, successful GVL is required to adopt innovative technologies and strategies to mitigate the challenges in GVTs for effective cooperation and performance.

First, based on prior VT research, to compensate for the lack of informal communication, GVL should actively promote regular interaction, social exchange, and the development of personal relationships with and among team members (Fajen, 2018; Jarvenpaa & Leidner, 1999; Zaccaro & Bader, 2003). These regular interactions build team identity and cohesion and further facilitate collective awareness while easing the potential of conflicts within GVTs (Mortensen &

[6] Trust in GVTs will receive particular attention in the following subsection (2.3.2) and will not be discussed in this section in detail.

Hinds, 2001). Building team cohesion is difficult under virtual conditions since there is no possibility, for example, to realize team-building activities on site or spontaneously go out for a meal or drink together after work without significant organizational effort (Fajen, 2018, p. 282).

Thus, GVL is required to overcome the lack of physical and informal interactions through regular electronic communication and, if possible, occasional face-to-face meetings of all GVT members (Fajen, 2018; Zander et al., 2013). GVL needs to guarantee a constant flow of communication and information to further collective awareness. Collective awareness refers to activity awareness, including team members' knowledge about the overall teamwork and various relevant contextual factors, and social awareness which refers to an exchange of private information (Daassi et al., 2010). By fostering collective awareness, global virtual leaders significantly reduce team members' insecurity and prevailing ambiguities while promoting trust and team cohesion. A constant update between GVT members and GVL, for example, about their work progress, and regular feedback from the leader and the team members are prerequisites for successful cooperation (Bergiel et al., 2008; Jarvenpaa & Leidner, 1999). GVL could thus adopt visualized tools that allow its members to stay aware of each other's timing, contribution, and activities, as suggested and developed by some VT experts (Glikson et al., 2019).[7] GVL could use CMC technologies that facilitate more nuanced expressions, such as video conferencing tools (Morrison-Smith & Ruiz, 2020). Additionally, GVL can employ a continuous virtual dialogue and curated virtual breaks for socializing between GVT members (Fajen, 2018, p. 281).

Additionally, Face-to-face encounters are highly recommended for successful team cooperation (Dubé & Robey, 2009). They boost mutual ties, trust, and understanding while enhancing awareness of others which is critical to preventing conflicts (Agerfalk et al., 2005; Armstrong & Cole, 1995). Face-to-face encounters are also associated with higher levels of consensus within groups, enhanced communication effectiveness, and greater efficiency in completing tasks (Gibson et al., 2014). Many VT researchers recommend that GVL organize face-to-face meetings when possible, particularly during the initial launch of a GVT, to create lasting bridges (Morrison-Smith & Ruiz, 2020).

Additionally, to further bridge the perceived and actual distance in GVTs, successful GVL needs to reduce the information gap and the feeling of isolation among team members (Fajen, 2018; O'Leary & Mortensen, 2010). GVL must ensure that relevant information is communicated evenly between team members

[7] Visualization tools can improve team effort and performance even in teams with low conscientious members (Glikson et al., 2019).

in different locations without granting any permanent information advantage to anybody. GVL should thus filter information and convey only the information pertinent to respective team members (Fajen, 2018, p. 275). To avoid team members feeling alone, especially in isolated sites, GVL should maintain regular bilateral exchanges with them—both via information and communication media as well as face-to-face. Most importantly, GVL is encouraged to engage intensively with all individual team members to respond to their personalities, use them according to their abilities, and take socio-cultural differences into account, for example, regarding communication. (Jarvenpaa & Leidner, 1999; Kayworth & Leidner, 2000).[8] Thus, successful GVL should constantly ask how their GVT members are doing and respond to their needs. GVT members should count on the leader's support in private and professional matters, especially in urgent matters (Fajen, 2018). GVL is encouraged to be very attentive and read between the lines to prevent misunderstandings and to recognize indications of issues within the team (Fajen, 2018).

Moreover, as communication difficulties lead to inefficient cooperation and team performance, GVL should ensure that relevant information is delivered adequately and is well understood by all GVT members (Dubé & Robey, 2009). Given the constraints on communication and reduced social context cues, GVTs and GVL must seek various means to transmit information, meaning, and symbols over time and space through one or more electronic channels (Fajen, 2018, pp. 81–82).[9] GVL should be aware that the success of GVTs depends upon the quality of the information available, how it is communicated and how the team members work together with this information to complete their tasks (Nydegger & Nydegger, 2010, p. 76). Thus, successful GVL should regularly reassure whether information has been received as intended.

Additionally, GVL is encouraged to incorporate essential cultural awareness and language training at the beginning of every project to mitigate communication effectiveness issues (Treinen & Miller-Frost, 2006). To reduce the effect of assumptions, GVL can employ agile development tools such as Scrum for daily status meetings or address issues or questions during the hand-off and allocation of tasks. Furthermore, regarding language barriers, GVL can encourage others to speak slowly and use a simple vocabulary (Fajen, 2018).

[8] GVL needs to develop a sense for the personalities present in the team, e.g. introverts and extroverts, and skills across the distance.

[9] GVTs and GVL could make use of emojis to transmit emotions.

Moreover, GVL is encouraged to create rules and norms for communication between team members early in the team's life cycle to increase effective communication and improve performance (Jarvenpaa & Leidner, 1999; Jawadi, 2013; Marlow et al., 2017). GVL should establish accepted and shared communication norms to build regular interaction patterns. Such norms enable GVL to construct a shared social context and team cohesion (Jawadi, 2013, p. 24). This is essential for managing highly complex tasks and avoiding misunderstandings due to high task complexity combined with high virtuality in GVTs (Marlow et al., 2017). GVL can employ closed feedback loops in communication that provide clarification opportunities to prevent misunderstandings.

Furthermore, successful GVL needs to provide adequate, functioning, and rich information and communication media for communication in GVTs to minimize communication issues and to maximize the potential for members to provide sufficient information for others (Fajen, 2018; Marlow et al., 2017; Morrison-Smith & Ruiz, 2020). However, GVL should be aware of the advantages and disadvantages of CMC and make proper use of the latter. CMC, such as asynchronous media (emails, texts), can reduce the negative effects of socio-cultural diversity and even be beneficial in GVTs (Morrison-Smith & Ruiz, 2020). Challenges regarding language barriers can be surmounted as GVT members can take their time to draft questions and responses, especially when the native language is not shared by all members (Holmstrom et al., 2006). The increased use of asynchronous media also comes with disadvantages, as this form of media takes more time and effort to effectively communicate (Agerfalk et al., 2005). It comes with that that GVL needs to ensure proper tech and media savviness of team members and itself (Fajen, 2018). It is therefore recommended to use several types of CMC media either concurrently (e.g., face-to-face communication accompanied by documents; telephone conferencing with synchronous electronic conferencing) or consecutively (e.g., conveying information via e-mail first, followed by con verging over the phone) (Morrison-Smith & Ruiz, 2020, p. 8).

Furthermore, with regards to communication issues related to temporal distance, this quote by a global virtual leader summarizes the central problem well:

> So it's like this: at a live meeting, typically one person is just about to go to bed, that's usually (laughter) the colleague in Shanghai, and the other is just kicked out of bed very early, that's the colleague in San Francisco. And that is a very, very big issue that should not be underestimated. (Fajen, 2018, p. 272)

GVL is required to determine the respective working hours of all members and a time frame for joint meetings even though there might be little overlap in working hours. GVL should not permanently induce team members to participate in joint virtual meetings very early or late and accept that some members will be less productive at given times (Fajen, 2018). GVL can offer, for instance, flexible work schedules or employ the 'follow-the-sun' concept where work is handed off at the end of the day in a one-time zone to workers beginning their day in another (Holmstrom et al., 2006; Treinen & Miller-Frost, 2006). If used efficiently, this method can be highly beneficial for employees and the company alike. However, it should be noted that the 'follow-the-sun' method requires additional oversight and time to facilitate the transfer of work from one team or team member to the other, bearing the potential for misunderstanding and conflicts (Treinen & Miller-Frost, 2006).[10]

Moreover, GVL needs to overcome the virtual distraction phenomenon (Fajen, 2018). This phenomenon occurs in telephone and video communication and has hardly been addressed in the scientific literature on global virtual teamwork. The danger of distraction is particularly significant, as team members can check e-mails, surf the Internet or pursue other activities unnoticed during a telephone and video call (Fajen, 2018, pp. 277–278). To minimize this issue, GVL must use video conferencing with excellent quality for important tasks and ask all team members to activate their video support at the beginning. Moreover, GVL can actively involve team members during virtual communication through regular polls or questions to prevent attention fading.[11]

Additionally, GVL must show a strong (virtual) presence (Fajen, 2018; Zigurs, 2003). Traditional team leaders have various ways to display their presence, including where they sit in meetings, body language, voice inflections, or their dress style (Zigurs, 2003, p. 344). However, the virtual context does not allow for the same presence. Thus, GVL needs to find new ways to make itself seen (Fajen, 2018; Zigurs, 2003). According to one global virtual leader of Fajen's research, the challenge relates to the following: "…even though you're not on-site, you still have to be there somehow. So you have to stay close to the people, keep in touch, and stay up to date and on the ball. I think that's the most challenging thing about it. " (Fajen, 2018, p. 279). GVL can show presence by quickly and regularly responding to GVT members' requests to demonstrate reliability.

[10] Another method is to limit the number of time zones in which sites are located.

[11] Leaders of GVTs should wisely choose the number of participants in telephone and video conferences so that a lively exchange is still possible. During communication, they should take into account the human attention span and avoid excessive presentations and discussions (Fajen, 2018, p. 279).

GVL should further maintain an open virtual door policy, i.e., make it clear to their team members that their leader is available and will assist its members at any time with advice and support. Additionally, GVL needs to learn how to use the vividness and interactivity of media to show virtual presence (Zigurs, 2003, p. 344). Rich and sophisticated videoconferencing tools which provide additional non-verbal cues and perceptible sensory signals are thus recommended (Fajen, 2018).

Furthermore, to overcome all the challenges in GVTs that hinder their effective employment and performance, GVL needs to put a lot of time and effort (Fajen, 2018). This effort is well summarized in the following quote from a global virtual leader: "I was on the phone last night until ten o'clock talking to guys in the U.S. I was on the phone at six-thirty this morning talking to guys in Asia." (Fajen, 2018, p. 274). GVL has to master numerous challenges while continually responding to the needs of socio-culturally diverse GVT members worldwide. Furthermore, many virtual leaders work in several teams simultaneously (Fajen, 2018). GVL should thus "schedule sufficient time in their day to make the calls, emails and online visits necessary to achieve an encompassing virtual walk around the entire team." (Bergiel et al., 2008, p. 105). Thus, to alleviate the time pressure and the high demands on GVL, thoughtful organization and coordination of the tasks are of the utmost importance.

In addition to the approaches mentioned in this chapter, the exercise of certain roles and tasks and good leadership behavior is necessary for virtual leaders to successfully meet the numerous challenges of leading GVTs. Thus, GVL is also required to have specific competencies and skills, which are addressed in the following chapter.

2.3.2 Specific Global Virtual Leadership Competences and Roles

This subsection will examine to what extent traditional leadership theories, styles, and concepts can be applied to a global virtual organizational context. It will further elucidate what specific global virtual leadership competencies and personality traits GVL should showcase, and which related roles it should fulfill to lead GVTs effectively.

First, one of the oldest leadership approaches is the trait theory of leadership, according to which personality traits and competencies influence leader emergence and effectiveness (Colbert et al., 2012; Fajen, 2018). According to most researchers in the field, these leadership qualities and abilities are not only innate but can also be learned through imprinting. The focus lies in a person's competence to act, which can be specifically trained in the professional environment through various measures, as well as on their social competencies, which means their ability to cooperate with people (Colbert et al., 2012; Fajen, 2018). Successful leadership competencies include the leader's aptitude, i.e., intelligence, responsibility, self-confidence, and reliability, organizational talent, communication skills, and empathy (Fajen, 2018; Von Rosenstiel, 2014). This correlative relationship between competencies and leadership success has been confirmed by numerous studies on virtual leadership (Fajen, 2018; Pierce & Hansen, 2008). More specifically, global virtual leaders should be honest and open (Fajen, 2018, p. 350), highly coordinated and structured, determined, motivated and diligent, and with a strong work ethic (Fajen, 2018, p. 352). Additionally, global (virtual) leaders need to have intercultural competencies to balance communication in GVTs and to accommodate potential misunderstandings due to socio-cultural differences that can lead to misunderstandings and miscommunication (cf. 2.2.3). As for balanced communication, GVL should, for example actively involve team members from indirect cultures in the conversation and occasionally slow down team members from direct cultures in their flow of speech to restore fairness and balance (Fajen, 2018).

Furthermore, the behavioral theory of leadership, which focuses on leadership behavior and style, finds resonance in the global virtual context (Daassi et al., 2010; Fajen, 2018). Behavior can be categorized according to the dimensions of task- and employee orientation (Daassi et al., 2007, 2010). Both are important to create collective awareness, which is essential for team cohesion and trust (Daassi et al., 2010). Through task-related functions like precise goal formulation and clear distribution of tasks, the leader creates an understanding of what is expected in the context of cooperation and who has which responsibilities, which refers to activity awareness. Employee-oriented functions include the building trust and team cohesion and promoting the exchange of private information among team members, referred to as social awareness (Daassi et al., 2010). By fostering collective awareness through both activity and social awareness, global virtual leaders contribute significantly to reducing the team members' insecurity and prevailing ambiguities, which are often prevalent due to the infrequent face-to-face contact in virtual teamwork (Fajen, 2018).

Moreover, concerning the behavioral complexity theory (BCT), leaders who operate in a complex environment characterized by contradictions must show the same degree of complexity in their behavior (Hooijberg, 1996). Thus, effective leadership behavior is characterized by behavioral complexity, which is "the ability to perform multiple roles and behaviors that circumscribe the requisite variety implied by an organizational or environmental context" (Hooijberg, 1996, p. 919). In this context, one can also refer to the "multidimensionality" of leadership behavior, which includes that leaders must follow a clear direction to be credible (Fajen, 2018).

As for the virtual context, there is a positive correlation between virtual leaders' exercise of different roles and their leadership effectiveness, which correlates positively with team success (Anawati & Craig, 2006; Fajen, 2018; Jawadi, 2013; Kayworth & Leidner, 2002). Thus, effective GVL exercises different leadership styles and roles simultaneously, even though sometimes contradictory but adapted to the respective context (Kayworth & Leidner, 2002). Moreover, effective cooperation between people from different cultural backgrounds can only work if they adjust their behavior, as the more significant their cultural differences, the more complicated the cooperation. This accounts especially for leaders of GVTs who have to accommodate the socio-cultural differences within the team (Anawati & Craig, 2006).GVL is thus required to exercise elements of transactional and transformational leadership (Anawati & Craig, 2006; Fajen, 2018).[12]

More specifically, successful GVL is advised to practice a result-oriented leadership style by constantly monitoring the outcomes of team members' individual and team outcomes while giving team members maximum flexibility in task completion (Fajen, 2018, p. 332). Even if leaders travel to the locations of the individual team members to get to know the team members and the respective local working conditions, they cannot possibly know all the details of the constantly changing conditions at the different locations. Nevertheless, they must make responsible decisions despite these information deficits (Fajen, 2018, p. 326). Thus, global virtual leaders have to transfer responsibility to their team (empowerment) to enable them to work independently and to motivate them. However, they also need to exercise control to ensure that team members are assigned the right tasks and maintain quality standards (Fajen, 2018).

Additionally, behavioral complexity correlates positively with reduced conflict in GVTs (Wakefield et al., 2008). If team members recognize different behavioral styles of their leader associated with the roles of mentor, supervisor, and supporter adapted to the respective context, conflicts within the team are reduced as these roles focus on optimizing team processes (Fajen, 2018; Wakefield et al., 2008). Most importantly, it has been shown that the quality of the relationship between

---

[12] Transactional leadership refers to a leadership style that focuses on supervision, organization, and performance including rewards and sanctions. Transformational leadership refers to a leadership style based on joint visions to guide change through influence and inspiration executed in concert in with committed members.

leader and team members and the level of trust in the team is positively influenced if the leader can assume different roles (Fajen, 2018; Jawadi, 2013).

Based on prior VT research on leadership tasks and roles (Kayworth & Leidner, 2002; Malhotra et al., 2007) and on behavioral complexity (Daassi et al., 2007, 2007; Hooijberg, 1996) as well as on Fajen's empirical research on successful GVL, Fajen has summarized all relevant findings and categorized them into twelve e-leader roles for successful GVL (Fajen, 2018, pp. 315–322). These include the roles of e-node, e-networker, e-organizer, e-coordinator, e-motivator, e-supporter, e-developer, e-controller, e-decision maker, e-responsible person, e-communicator and e-trust promoter and will be elaborated briefly in the following paragraphs.

First, global virtual leaders have to fulfill the role of *e-node*. The leader must have a "view of the whole" and maintain an overview of the activities of all colleagues, given the communication challenges. Regular interaction with all team members means the team leader has extensive information and can act as the central point of contact (Fajen, 2018, pp. 315–322).

Second, to bridge the perceived distance between the leader and team members and to ensure a continuous flow of communication, GVL needs to take on the role of *e-networker*. GVL should therefore ensure that the geographically dispersed team members meet regularly, both virtually and face-to-face, to build trust and team cohesion to create a solid foundation for global virtual cooperation (Fajen, 2018, pp. 315–322).

Third, global virtual leaders need to fulfill the roles of *e-organizer* and *e-coordinator*. Virtual leaders must realize complex organizational and coordination tasks, including creating common and individual goals and transnational visions, developing strategies, setting priorities, virtual team meetings, and so forth (Fajen, 2018, pp. 315–322).

Forth, another essential role of global virtual leaders is being an *e-motivator*. As such, they must drive the team members to fulfill their goals. They must inspire, convince, and show them respect and appreciation. A particularly efficient form of motivation in GVTs is to grant team members freedom in their work and to give them responsibility (empowerment), as this expresses the leader's trust in the team (Fajen, 2018, pp. 315–322).

Fifth, as *e-supporter* global virtual leaders are required to help with both professional and private problems of their team members. Global virtual team members who find themselves alone at their location and who are confronted with issues have to be able to rely on their leader (Fajen, 2018, pp. 315–322).

Moreover, as *e-developer* global virtual leaders have to ensure the continuous development of each team member; virtual team members should have the possibility for lifelong learning to unfold their potential. They should be able to continuously receive new virtual team training, including tailor-made training measures adapted to the respective needs of each team member (Fajen, 2018, pp. 315–322).

Additionally, global virtual leaders are required to exercise the role of an *e-controller*. This includes checking whether the team members perform their tasks adequately and on time. The evaluation of individual and team performance and the promotion of desired or prevention of undesired behavior are also part of the control task and give the team members orientation (Fajen, 2018, pp. 315–322).

Furthermore, *as e-decision-maker* and *e-responsibility-maker*, global virtual leaders are in charge of creating consensus within the team and, if necessary, making the final decision while bearing the responsibility for it. They should have the necessary expertise, including all relevant information, e.g., available resources and higher-level corporate goals (Fajen, 2018, pp. 315–322).

Furthermore, GVL should fulfill the role of *e-communicator*. This is an essential part of all the roles mentioned above. GVL should have exceptional communication skills, including intercultural competencies, and be able to express itself in straightforward language, both orally and in writing to ensure adequate communication of goals and expectations across locations and cultures. The following tasks are part of this particular role: giving constructive feedback, combining personal knowledge of team members, promoting knowledge transfer within the team, and regular exchange and interaction within GVTs.

Finally, successful GVL is required to take on the particular role of an *e-trust promoter* (Fajen, 2018, p. 318). Global virtual leaders must promote the 'swift trust' usually present at the beginning of virtual teamwork and support the development of longstanding mutual trust in the team. Regular contact via the richest possible information and communication media is essential and intense relationship building to achieve this goal. According to Fajen, this is a specific role in and for global virtual team leadership which will find further attention in this thesis.

To sum, GVTs present unique challenges due to their spatial, temporal, and structural dispersion superseded by the socio-cultural differences in the team. Their effective employment demands less management but more leadership and explicit (virtual) leadership competencies and skills. This high degree of complexity requires leadership to exercise multiple roles and leadership styles which is evidence of the indispensability of leadership in GVTs (Fajen, 2018, p. 331). Consequently, the trust creation process is more difficult in GVTs. The following subsection will further elucidate this point and elaborate on how GVL can promote trust in GVT.

2.3.3 Trust as Fundamental Condition for Leading Effective Global Virtual Teams

This subsection shows that while building trust is the main challenge for GVL in GVTs, it is also a fundamental condition for effective leadership. Based on previous VT research, this subsection will further elaborate on how GVL can promote trust in GVTs to guarantee team effectiveness and cooperation (Daassi et al., 2010; Fajen, 2018; Jarvenpaa et al., 2004; Jarvenpaa & Leidner, 1999; Jawadi, 2013). Due to the leadership topic of this thesis, the following focuses on interpersonal trust, i.e., trust in persons. In addition to trust in the leader, the leader's trust in the team members and of the team members in each other is also taken into account (Fajen, 2018).

Trust refers to the confidence that the behavior of another will conform to one's expectations and in the goodwill of another (Ring & Van de Ven, 1994). Consequently, trusted parties should stick to agreements, be honest and not take advantage of their counterparts (Fajen, 2018; Ring & Van de Ven, 1994; Suchanek, 2015).[13] However, due to specific characteristics of the virtual context, the establishment and development of trust are hampered (Hacker et al., 2019). Even though trust mechanisms largely intercept with those of traditional, face-to-face teams due to different time zones, nationalities and cultures, working styles, and languages, it is more challenging for GVTs to work together effectively and to build trust (Ford et al., 2017, pp. 3–5).

Face-to-face interactions and physical proximity, which contribute to interpersonal relationship development and thus trust building, are limited in GVTs and superseded by the heavy use of CMC media, which lacks verbal cues and facial expressions (Jawadi, 2013; Townsend et al., 1998). Research has shown, however, that observing others largely impacts the ability to trust (Ford et al., 2017; Mayer et al., 1995). Thus, due to GVTs virtuality, including its spatial, temporal, and structural dispersion trust, is fragile as GVTs represent limited relationship-building opportunities (Townsend et al., 1998).

This difficulty in establishing trust profoundly affects collaboration and performance in GVTs (Fajen, 2018; Ford et al., 2017; Hacker et al., 2019; Jarvenpaa & Leidner, 1999; Jawadi, 2013). This reduced trust will interfere with work performance, resulting in lower employee support of leadership while negatively impacting the adjustments to the virtual work environment (Merriman et al.,

[13] Section 3.1 and 3.2. will elaborate more in detail on the topic of trust, specifically in relations to GVTs and GVL.

2007). More specifically, this reduced trust can lead to corrosion of task coordination (Morrison-Smith & Ruiz, 2020; Olson & Olson, 2011). As summarized by Morrison and Ruiz (2020), reduced trust in GVTs can lead to decreased eagerness to communicate and a lack of empathy for teammates. Furthermore, a lack of trust inhibits team members from coping with unstructured tasks and uncertainty. It further reduces their willingness to take the initiative and give proactive feedback to teammates (Jarvenpaa & Leidner, 1999). Moreover, some VT studies have shown that decreased trust in GVTs impacts team cohesion negatively, with team members not feeling belonging to one team (Kotlarsky & Oshri, 2005; O'Leary & Mortensen, 2010). Thus, as a consequence, GVTs often lack strong professional and personal relationships common to traditional teams (Jarvenpaa & Leidner, 1999). These issues have detrimental effects on collaboration and performance in GVTs, with regularly occurring project delays and failure (Morrison-Smith & Ruiz, 2020, p. 6).

Even though the use of face-to-face encounters has been identified as having an irreplaceable role in building and repairing trust, most VT researchers agree however that through the use of modern technologies, social spheres where trust between the leader and the team members can be built can still emerge in virtual spaces (Jarvenpaa et al., 2004; Jarvenpaa & Leidner, 1999).[14] Though trust development is suggested as the main challenge in GVTs, most VT researchers agree that interpersonal trust among GVT members is a necessary prerequisite to solving communication, technological and cultural challenges (Hacker et al., 2019, p. 2). According to some VT authors, trust is even more critical in GVTs than in co-located teams because of their geographical dispersion and their heavy use of CMC (Robert et al., 2009, p. 242). The accumulating research across a range of disciplines, among them management, psychology, computer sciences, and communication, have identified trust as the heart of virtual team functioning and as one of the fundamental critical factors for successful virtual collaboration (Breuer et al., 2016; Fajen, 2018; Ford et al., 2017; Jarvenpaa et al., 2004; Jawadi, 2013; Kanawattanachai & Yoo, 2002; Wilson et al., 2006). The importance of trust in GVTs will be analyzed in depth in the following chapters of 3.1.

Previous VT research concludes that GVL plays a significant role in fostering interpersonal trust in their teams (Ford et al., 2017; Hacker et al., 2019; Jarvenpaa & Leidner, 1999; Kayworth & Leidner, 2000). Effective leaders develop

---

[14] Team members can sometimes even convey more emotions and develop greater familiarity with each other in virtual interaction than in face-to-face cooperation, since more time is allocated from the outset for individuals to introduce themselves and get to know each other than in ordinary face-to-face meetings (Fajen, 2018, pp. 84–85).

high levels of trust in their teams, resulting in enhanced virtual team performance (Jawadi, 2013, p. 19). Prior research agrees that trust-building requires an active involvement and promotion by GVL (Fajen, 2018, p. 104). Thus, GVL is responsible for further fortifying and enhancing the given swift trust in GVTs Thus, to build trust, GVL should establish common goals, a transnational vision, and define tasks clearly (Jarvenpaa & Leidner, 1999). In this regard, key behaviors leading to high trust in GVTs include proactive actions, goal clarity, task focus, fast and positive feedback, and rotating leadership (Jawadi, 2013, p. 20).

Regarding goal clarity, building a sense of shared goals takes more time in distance collaboration (Armstrong & Cole, 1995). Moreover, aligning goals between all members is difficult to realize in a virtual context and requires substantial negotiation (Morrison-Smith & Ruiz, 2020; Olson & Olson, 2000). However, the extent to which virtual team members share common goals is critical in determining the team's success (Cho, 2006). Successful GVL should therefore have the capacity for the "rational pursuit of goals" (Jawadi, 2013). Team leaders should ensure that team members commit to shared goals and defined tasks. Especially in the initial phase of cooperation in GVTs, it is conducive if team leaders motivate team members to communicate their enthusiasm for achieving common goals, encourage each other in this way, clarify technical problems right at the beginning of the cooperation, ensure a common understanding of the task content and show a high degree of initiative (Fajen, 2018; Jarvenpaa & Leidner, 1999). GVL needs to remove any uncertainty about the task by providing specific performance feedback to the team on progress while setting and monitoring deadlines and holding team members individually and collectively accountable for performance (Kirkman et al., 2004). The defined team tasks should further be linked to a common team mission and transnational vision to gain team members' trust (Ford et al., 2017, p. 5).[15]

Moreover, to foster trust GVL should promote frequent communication and regular interactions between all GVT members and itself (Jarvenpaa et al., 2004; Jarvenpaa & Leidner, 1999). To compensate for the lack of formal and informal communication and exchange in GVTs, GVL has to actively promote regular exchange and guarantee a constant flow of information necessary for building trust. While communication in traditional teams often takes place unconsciously or independently, digital communication must be consciously initiated. Thus, it is always essential to reflect on which information and communication medium

[15] The more specific the leader can make every team members' tasks, roles, and responsibilities, the easier it will be to communicate through a common performance metric that keeps everyone focused on where the team is and how it is doing on reaching its goal (Ford et al., 2017, p. 8).

is most suitable for the current occasion (Fajen, 2018, pp. 324–325). Through continuous and frequent interaction, team members can build a sense of closeness independent of physical proximity (Morrison-Smith & Ruiz, 2020). Previous VT research has linked trust positively to team awareness (Daassi et al., 2007; Jawadi, 2013). As elaborated in the last chapter, GVL can further collective team awareness through activity and social awareness, which considerably reduces the team members' insecurity and prevailing ambiguities (cf. 2.3.1, cf. 2.3.2)(Daassi et al., 2007). Thus, GVL can contribute to creating team cohesion and a team spirit despite geographical distribution, which is of the utmost importance for trust (Fajen, 2018).

Additionally, trust needs to be reinforced through ongoing interpersonal relationship experiences (Ford et al., 2017, p. 3). Thus, while task-related roles are essential for trust-building, GVL should underpin relationship-oriented functions and encourage human relationship-building in GVTs (Fajen, 2018; Jawadi, 2013).[16] While task-oriented roles focus on solving tasks efficiently and responsibly, relationship-oriented parts concentrate primarily on improving the quality of the relationship between the leader and the team members or between the team members, thus increasing the motivation of the team members and developing their skills (Fajen, 2018). Task-oriented roles can contain relationship-oriented aspects and vice versa.[17] Moreover, as lack of trust is most pronounced during the initial stage of GVT collaboration, GVL should promote social information exchanges early on in the life of a project (Jarvenpaa & Leidner, 1999). GVL can further boost the trust creation process in GVTs by encouraging the exchange of task-related information and personal information (Fajen, 2018, p. 104).

In line with that, GVL should use mechanisms and establish practices to increase the level of awareness in GVTs to build trusty relationships (Jawadi, 2013, p. 20). GVL can employ creative solutions of virtual get-togethers and encourage the active participation of GVT members (Ford et al., 2017, p. 5). GVL could create socializing opportunities for casual interactions between all GVT members, for example, by employing virtual dialogues (Fajen, 2018, p. 281). Moreover, GVL is advised to use punctual face-to-face encounters for trust-building. Especially an initial face-to-face meeting at the beginning of virtual collaboration has been shown to impact the trust level positively in GVTs (Jarvenpaa & Leidner, 1999; Marlow et al., 2017).

---

16 If team members in GVTs mainly exchange task-related information, this creates uncertainty about the motivation of colleagues and their efforts to achieve team goals.

17 Fajen's research concludes that while both task- and relationship-oriented roles are important, overall, the relationship-oriented roles of GVL have slightly more weight as they positively influence tasks (Fajen, 2018).

Moreover, to build trust, GVL needs to ensure a continual flow of information necessary for GVT members to fulfill their tasks and to help them stay aware of the accomplishments of organizational matters and other team members (Ford et al., 2017; Kayworth & Leidner, 2000; Kayworth & Leidner, 2002). As there are no coffee hall encounters, GVL needs to fill in this gap and provide extra information necessary for the trust-building process in GVTs (Ford et al., 2017, p. 7). GVT members often feel that 'out of sight' leads to 'out of mind.' Thus, GVL should often communicate to all members individually and collectively about the task, what the contribution of each member is expected to play for the accomplishment of the overall team goals, how these goals are means to the organizational mission, and what progress is being made (Ford et al., 2017; Kayworth & Leidner, 2000). In this regard, GVL should recognize and value individual accomplishments to grant its members psychological safety (Ford et al., 2017; Hertel et al., 2005). GVL is thus the visible and effective cheerleader for both the team and all team members (Ford et al., 2017, p. 8).

Furthermore, GVL supporting its members' social-emotional needs is vital to building trust (Ford et al., 2017, p. 5). GVL must have a strong employee orientation and pay special attention to the socio-emotional needs of their members (Fajen, 2018, pp. 325–326). Socio-emotional processes such as motivation, commitment, and contentment are intrinsically linked to each other and especially to trust (Fajen, 2018).[18] The socio-cultural background of the team members largely influences their motivation. Although all people have basic biological needs in common, such as the need for food, an individual's culture considerably affects the development of other needs and their ranking (Fajen, 2018). Important determinants are the values underlying culture and the socialization a person undergoes. Whereas U.S. Americans generally place a high value on individual needs, Japanese people have a greater need to achieve a high social status (Fajen, 2018, pp. 110–111). GVL should be aware of these cultural differences and must have intercultural competencies to accommodate the socio-emotional needs of its GVT members (cf. 2.3.2).

Besides, GVL needs to provide the necessary technological infrastructure as the effectiveness, reliability, and usefulness of the CMC media affect the trust-building process (Choi & Cho, 2019; Morrison-Smith & Ruiz, 2020) GVTs depend on having appropriate communication technology to connect and support the members in ways that develop trust (Ford et al., 2017, p. 4). Organizations

[18] The empirically validated VIST model (Hertel et al., 2004) shows how motivation processes in virtual teamwork parallels to the motivation processes in traditional face-to-face teams.

send cues to their teams through the quality of the technology provided. CMC should thus be reliable, rich, and fast as necessary to properly perform the communication functions required by the team (Ford et al., 2017, p. 4). It comes with that that GVL and GVT members should be media and tech-savvy (Fajen, 2018; Ford et al., 2017; Jawadi, 2013). Based on the media naturalness perspective (DeRosa et al., 2004), it is difficult for members to trust when communicating electronically. However, once they have learned to use CMC properly and have developed communication routines, it becomes easier for teams to build trusty relationships (Jawadi, 2013, p. 20). Additionally, GVT members' perceptions of their leaders and other members' level of media and tech savviness further influence the trust relationship. GVL should thus provide technology training and technological support for their teams while ensuring their level of proficiency (Ford et al., 2017, p. 3).

Further, GVL should adequately select and prepare GVT members as team composition plays a crucial role in trust-building (Ford et al., 2017, pp. 4–5). GVL should be aware that some people are more able to work in GVTs than others. Even though team members' expertise to achieve the team's mission is crucial for GVT success, other factors that influence team success and especially trust relate to people's personality characteristics and personal values (Ford et al., 2017, p. 9). Thus, GVT member's willingness to trust and a positive view of the organization (Ford et al., 2017, p. 9) as well as their integrity, competence, fairness, honesty, openness, and level of autonomy in their respective teams influence trust in GVTs (Choi & Cho, 2019).

In line with that, GVL's competencies for trust-building should also include GVL's capacity to adapt its leadership style to different contexts while establishing personal relationships with all members(Fajen, 2018)[19]. The quality of the relationship between the leader and their team members, as well as the level of trust existing in the team, is positively influenced if the leader can assume different roles (cf. 2.2.2). Trust in GVTs not only develops through task-related actions but also positive and dynamic behaviors (Jawadi, 2013, p. 22). As elaborated in the previous chapter GVL is required to showcase behavioral complexity. Effectively managing complex and ambiguous situations through behavior adaptation has positively impacted trust within the GVTs (Fajen, 2018; Jawadi, 2013).

Additionally, GVL should work towards conceptualizing shared leadership to promote trust in GVTs (Ford et al., 2017; Hoch & Kozlowski, 2014). Due to a lack of physical presence, effective leadership is complex (cf. 2.3.1). Thus, the team has to be empowered to fill in any gaps and substitute direct leadership

[19] Subchapter 2.3.2 summarizes these competences and roles.

(Ford et al., 2017, p. 4). Traditional supervisory monitoring and oversight methods undermine virtual team effectiveness. Thus, control needs to be replaced by trust to breed more trust in the team (Ford et al., 2017, p. 6). Successful GVL gives its team members decision-making power and thus empowers them so that they achieve the best possible performance. However, GVT members who appear to be self-leading but only solve problems and lack authority to make their own decisions lead the team members to mistrust GVL (Morrison-Smith & Ruiz, 2020). Thus, GVL should fully engage their team members and grant them authority and responsibility. GVL can do this through training in shared leadership strategies while developing clear plans, policies, and procedures that define tasks and how these tasks should be performed (Ford et al., 2017, p. 6; Hoch & Kozlowski, 2014).

Finally, of particular importance for this dissertation are the two following points that will receive further detailed attention in the following subsections (3.2.2, 3.2.3, 3.3). First, global virtual leaders must act as role models or at least should be perceived as role models for trust in GVTs (Fajen, 2018, p. 333). Second, trust in GVTs requires some sort of common ground concerning communication between the leader and all members.[20] Shared (team) mental models (SMMs) are a prime example of common ground in GVTs (Schmidtke & Cummings, 2017).[21]

Overall, this subsection has shown that while trust represents the biggest challenge for GVL, building trust is also the most fundamental task of GVL for effective GVT cooperation and performance. Trust supports GVL in overcoming the temporal, spatial, and structural differences in GVTs and their resulting challenges regarding communication, technology use, and socio-cultural differences. Given the lack of frequent face-to-face interactions or informal communication, the trust creation process in GVT represents itself as more difficult than in co-located teams. Thus, GVL is required to actively promote the trust-building process in GVTs. GVL can promote professional and personal exchange in GVTs by fostering collective team awareness through raising activity and social awareness. GVL has to fulfill the various task and employee-related functions for trust and specifically further human relationship building, to create team cohesion and trust. Thus, choosing adequate GVT members and competent and skillful GVL

[20] Common ground refers to that knowledge that the members have in common, and they are aware that they have it in common (Clark, 1996).

[21] Shared (team) mental models are a common understanding of team knowledge that members have regarding their tasks and the way they need to interact in order to accomplish these (Converse et al., 1993; Maynard & Gilson, 2014, p. 4)

with a proven track record of success has been established to further trust in GVTs (Ford et al., 2017, p. 4).

The following subsection will introduce the research gap and contribution of this thesis.

2.4 The Research Gap and Contribution

While the last subchapter has defined trust as the fundamental condition for leading effective GVTs for effective cooperation and performance (cf. 2.3.3), this subchapter will introduce a business ethical perspective on trust, GVTs, and GVL while identifying the research gap to demonstrate how this thesis contributes with new knowledge to academic literature. Moreover, this thesis's hypothesis and academic contributions concerning how global virtual leaders can promote trust in GVTs will be brought forward. Thus, the findings of chapter 2 are summarized in a new conceptual model to broaden the understanding of GVL and its impact on creating trust in GVTs by offering an interdisciplinary perspective.

While most VT researchers agree that trust is a fundamental condition for successful GVTs based on effective cooperation and performance, they further argue that trust research in VT requires much more attention (Fajen, 2018; Hacker et al., 2019; Jawadi, 2013; Morrison-Smith & Ruiz, 2020). Although previous work offers essential insights into trust-building mechanisms in GVTs (Crisp & Jarvenpaa, 2013; Ford et al., 2017; Hacker et al., 2019; Jarvenpaa et al., 2004; Jarvenpaa & Leidner, 1999), several gaps remain especially with regards to the role of leadership on trust-building.

First, global virtual leadership and trust have been explored at a very general level. Prior research has focused on leadership competencies, characteristics, styles, and personality traits that foster trust in GVTs (Ford et al., 2017). However, there is a lack of research concerning actions and practices that GVL can employ to actively promote and sustain trust in socio-cultural diverse GVTs. Previous research advises GVL to promote face-to-face encounters, regular interaction, and social information exchange (Fajen, 2018, p. 106) and to create rules for communication (Jarvenpaa & Leidner, 1999; Jawadi, 2013) fails, however, to give concrete clues about how effective communication should look like to overcome the communication effectiveness challenges that impede the development of trust. Additionally, to date, little is known about how leaders can encourage the building of trust from a socio-emotional perspective in GVTs despite encouraging face-to-face encounters, regular interaction, and social information exchange (Fajen, 2018; Jarvenpaa & Leidner, 1999; Kayworth & Leidner, 2002).

Moreover, even though diversity in the form of socio-cultural differences between virtual team members has been found to impede the development of trust in GVTs due to regular miscommunication, biases, and conflicts (Gibson & Manuel, 2003, p. 67), prior VT research does not offer many detailed options of how to overcome challenges related to socio-cultural distance. Previous research suggests o introduce clear communication rules in GVTs (Jarvenpaa & Leidner, 1999; Jawadi, 2013) fails, however, to give more concrete cues about how these communication rules should look like explicitly to create trust in a socio-cultural diverse context.

In line with that, prior VT research on trust in GVTs fails to develop how trust relationships and mutual trust expectations are formed in GVTs, especially concerning socio-cultural differences among team members. There is also no research on how GVL can support building mutual trust expectations with regard to socio-cultural differences.

Furthermore, the concept of common ground[22] as a condition for trust and effective cooperation has been introduced by VT literature as of the utmost importance (Jarvenpaa & Leidner, 1999; Zolin et al., 2004). Moreover, as an example of common ground, shared (team) mental models (SMMs)[23] regarding the team and tasks have been further introduced (Maynard & Gilson, 2014; Schmidtke & Cummings, 2017). However, prior research has failed to deconstruct the respective elements of an SMM that ultimately leads to trust, especially concerning the formation of mutual trust expectations in socio-cultural diverse GVTs.

Finally, prior VT research on GVTs, GVL, and trust emanates mainly from the realm of management sciences, including intercultural management, social sciences such as sociology and (social) psychology, as well as communication and information sciences. A business ethical perspective and a normative approach to GVT, leadership, and trust are still lacking. Fajen's research even concludes that to date, no research has looked into the influence of ethical leadership behavior on socio-emotional processes such as trust and the influence of ethical values on behavior rules for GVTs (Fajen, 2018, p. 371).

VT research generally agrees that further research needs to address trust, leadership, and collaboration in GVTs (Robert Jr & You, 2018, p. 25), especially concerning adequate communication methods that create a sustainable trust for effective cooperation and performance (Morrison-Smith & Ruiz, 2020, p. 7).

[22] Common ground refers to that knowledge that the members have in common, and they are aware that they have it in common (Clark, 1996).

[23] Shared (team) mental models are a common understanding of team knowledge that members have regarding their tasks and the way they need to interact in order to accomplish these (Converse et al., 1993; Maynard & Gilson, 2014, p. 4).

Thus, this thesis aims to close these research gaps by introducing a business ethical and normative perspective on trust, GVTs, and GVL while merging prior VT literature with new conceptual models that give GVL a practical guide to creating and sustaining trust in socio-culturally diverse GVTs. As of that, the research question of this thesis can be derived: *how can GVL actively promote trust and create common ground regarding mutual reliable trust expectations in socio-culturally diverse GVTs?*

This thesis hypothesizes that GVL can actively create trust in GVTs by investing in trust through realizing the ethical focal point do no (illegitimate) harm based on the good leadership model by Suchanek (2019). The ethical focal point do no (illegitimate) harm can serve as common ground regarding mutual reliable trust expectations in socio-culturally diverse GVTs. This thesis solely focuses on how GVL can promote trust in socio-culturally diverse GVTs concerning mutual trust expectations. This thesis will not focus on the trust-building process with other third parties. There will be no further reference to the above explanation of the research topic and focus.

This thesis answers the research question by creating synergies between normative business ethics and current GVT literature concerning trust-building. Based on this, the thesis will derive practical implementation advice for global virtual team leaders on how to promote and sustain trust in GVTs for effective cooperation and performance. Thus, the findings of chapter 2 are summarized in a new conceptual model to broaden the understanding of GVL and its impact on creating trust in GVTs by offering an interdisciplinary perspective. The following paragraph will elucidate how this thesis will prove the hypothesis and thus contribute new knowledge to the general study of GVTs, GVL, and trust.

The first contribution of this thesis is the introduction of the business ethical concept of the ethical focal point do no (illegitimate) harm for trust (3.1.2, 3.1.3). The golden rule's do no harm principle will be elucidated as the central and necessary condition for trust in (global virtual) teams for long-term social cooperation (Suchanek 2008). Moreover, after elucidating focal points as points of orientation, the ethical focal point do no (illegitimate) harm will be introduced as the primary point of orientation to align respective trust expectations and actions (Suchanek & Entschew, 2018) (3.1.3, 3.2.1). This new conceptual model allows for a better understanding of the trust creation process in GVTs, especially regarding the formation of mutual trust expectations.

Moreover, this research contributes to the research on shared mental models (SMMs) and, more particularly, on shared mental model (SMM) similarity in GVTs (Schmidtke & Cummings, 2017) by proposing the ethical focal point do no (illegitimate) harm as shared (team) mental model (3.2.1) to align trust expectations and actions in socio-culturally diverse GVTs (3.2.1). It will further be shown that trust needs a shared understanding regarding the illegitimacy of harm (Suchanek, 2015), especially relevant in GVTs due to their socio-culturally diversity.

Third, this thesis introduces the practical syllogism as a tool to merge normative and empirical levels to derive relevant courses of action and expectations (Suchanek, 2015, pp. 41–53) regarding how GVL can build trust in GVTs. Consisting of three consecutive orders on which the structure of chapter 3 is based, the practical syllogism conveys ethics with realism (Suchanek, 2015).

Moreover, this dissertation contributes to new knowledge by introducing a practical tool for GVL to implement trust in GVTs based on the good leadership model of Suchanek (2019). Relevant prior VT key findings will be integrated with regards to the four elements of that model, namely 1) the attitude of respect, 2) giving orientation by creating an SMM of do no (illegitimate) harm, 3) setting adequate framework conditions for trust and 4) GVL as a role model. This thesis aims to enrich the definition of GVL's role as an e-trust promoter (Fajen, 2018, p. 319).

Finally, this thesis will demonstrate the application of some elements of the good leadership model for trust in a real-life case illustration for the company Think-it (Think-it, 2022) for which a tailor-made leadership seminar was created (Avantgardist Institut, 2021).

In sum, Chapter 2 has elaborated on GVTs, GVL, and trust based on key findings of previous VT research. After elaborating a working definition of GVTs and GVL (cf. 2.1), it has been shown that GVTs have been on the rise due to several key trends since the 1970 s concerning communication and technological advancements (cf. 2.2.1). Superseded by the globalization and the internationalization of organizations industry and policy are increasingly employing GVTs in all kind of sectors, especially for strategic tasks and service-intense products. While virtual work bears a variety of benefits for companies and employees alike, the employment of GVTs is equally challenging due to their spatial, temporal and structural dispersion and further dimensions of virtuality (cf. 2.2.2). More specifically these challenges related to communication, the use of technology and socio-cultural differences can impact cooperation and performance negatively in GVTs (cf. 2.2.3). Furthermore, it has been shown that adequate GVL is of the utmost importance in GVTs to overcome all the challenges in order to ensure effective collaboration and performance (cf. 2.3.1). Successful GVL needs to fulfil a variety of sometimes even contradicting roles while having specific leadership competencies and personality traits to be adequately equipped to ensure the proper functioning and cooperation of GVTs (cf. 2.3.2). Furthermore, trust has been elucidated as fundamental condition for leading successful GVTs for effective cooperation and performance (cf. 2.3.3). It has been shown that GVL can build trust in GVTs by enhancing collective awareness and employing a variety of task-related and employee-related actions.

3 Bringing in Trust into Global Virtual Leadership

The objective of chapter 3 is to merge current GVT literature from the previous chapter 2 with business ethical concepts regarding trust, GVTs, and GVL. Chapter 3 is structured based on the heuristical tool of the practical syllogism, which will be further explained in the following paragraph. Section 3.1 will answer why trust is a fundamental condition for successful interactions in GVTs and show how business ethical concepts can shed light on this matter. Furthermore, section 3.2. summarizes the challenges to trust-building in GVTs concerning different trust expectations and the importance for GVL to role model trustworthiness. Finally, section 3.3 will answer the research question by showing how GVL can realize trust in GVTs by applying the business ethical tool of the good leadership model (Suchanek, 2019). Chapter 3 closes with section 3.4, the case illustration of this thesis.

> Teams of people working together for a common purpose have been a centerpiece of human social organization ever since our ancient ancestors first banded together to hunt game, raise families, and defend their communities. Human history is largely a story of people working together in groups to explore, achieve, and conquer. (Kozlowski & Ilgen, 2006, p. 77)

This quote counts specifically for GVTs that are growing in importance for industry and policy alike. Therefore, leading GVTs successfully means ensuring their effective cooperation and performance. Cooperation, in general, is based on successful interactions between individuals or entities and is thus a condition for the functioning of our everyday life (Suchanek, 2015, p. 54). Generally speaking, cooperation is based on the premise that the cooperating parties contribute to achieving the desired result (Suchanek, 2015, p. 87). Moreover, individuals are subject to these interactions are in a mutual dependency to realize cooperation.

L. Jassemi, *Global Virtual Teams & Trust*, Gabler Theses,
https://doi.org/10.1007/978-3-658-41852-6_3

As individuals are free to act, they are always subject to the freedom of action of others. It is precisely this freedom that allows individuals either to work in a way to gain cooperative gains or not (Suchanek, 2015).

Moreover, individuals are embedded in social and societal empirical realities engendering many conditions that might prevent cooperation, such as contradictory incentives, misunderstandings, a lack of information, weak will, budget restrictions, competition, and emotional barriers. These constraints are closely related to the *willingness* and *ability* of the cooperation partners (Suchanek, 2015, p. 87). Thus, concerning cooperation, this potential lack of mutual reliability in social interactions represents the core problem (Suchanek, 2015). Based on an Aristotelean-inspired theory of business, Solomon inquires about the importance of cooperation for social life. He stresses the related virtues of honesty, fairness, compassion, and trust in the competitive business world (Solomon, 1992). Trust offers a solution to overcome these (social) dilemma structures (Balliet & Van Lange, 2013), if it is justified and honored (De Biasi, 2019; Suchanek, 2015). Trust is essential to social relationships and allows for mutual cooperative relationships (Balliet & Van Lange, 2013; Deutsch, 1958) despite the risk that cooperation might not work out, and one party may benefit at the cost of the other (Suchanek, 2015, p. 61).

Moreover, ethics as a scientific theory of morality aims to assess and/or recommend (morally justified) actions. The practical syllogism which serves as the overall structure of chapter 3 is a crucial instrument for deriving such actions (Homann, 2014). This tool was already brought forward by Aristoteles in his Nichomachean Ethics and coined as a form of practical reason. Moreover, within the realm of business ethics, Homann grants great importance to this heuristic tool and refers to the fact that the goodwill of an individual to take moral actions is not enough but has to be brought together with the reality of facts (Homann, 2014, pp. 13–14). Thus, the practical syllogism represents the principal problem of everyday (business) ethics: to make moral judgments by reflecting the relation of values and reality, of *should* and *is* including shared goals and interests and the conditions of their realization. As a useful tool guiding practical reason, the practical syllogism combines *willingness* and *ability* and *normative* and *empirical* statements systematically (Suchanek, 2015, p. 42).

Thus, referring to the structure of the practical syllogism, chapter 3 is broken down as follows:

1) It starts with the preliminary question, *"What do I/want?"* referring to foundational goals and values and concerning this thesis to cooperation for mutual

advantage (Suchanek, 2015, p. 48).[1] Subchapter 3.1. will elaborate a working definition of interpersonal trust and elucidate why trust is the key to successful interactions. It will further clarify the different specificities of trust and its function and consequences in GVTs.

2) The second question refers to the empirical reality and asks, "*What am I/we able to do?*". This question relates to the multitude of empirical constraints like money, resources, time, market competition, and so forth interfering with the realization of (1) values, intentions, and goals (Suchanek, 2015, p. 43).[2] Thus, subchapter 3.2 elaborates on the challenges to trust-building in GVTs regarding different trust expectations existent in GVTs, the problem of a lack of a shared mental model regarding the illegitimacy of harm, and the role-modeling function of GVL for trust.
3) The integration between (1) and (2) results in what one ought to do and refers to the level of actions. It answers the question, *"What should I//we do?"*. Thus, the practical syllogism implies that a chosen course of action should reflect values and willingness (1) and the possibilities and ability given by the situation (2). The degree of individual freedom depends on the willingness and ability of the individual and how they deal with the given situational conditions (Suchanek, 2015, p. 43). Regarding GVTs, subchapter 3.3 shows that GVL needs to invest in the core condition of trust, namely the *ethical focal point do no (illegitimate) harm.* GVL can do so by realizing *do no (illegitimate) harm* based on Suchanek's model of good leadership (2019), which consists of four dimensions, namely 1) showing respect, 2) creation of a shared understanding with regards to the illegitimacy of harm 3) setting adequate framework conditions and 4) GVL as a role model for trustworthiness. As part of the 3rd order of the practical syllogism, subchapter 3.4 adds a practical example of the realization of the good leadership model based on the company Think-It.

---

[1] Given the diversity of peoples' interests, goals and values, there is a potential for inconsistency. The practical syllogism helps to prioritize these on focusing on 'why' certain priorities should be set (Suchanek, 2015, p. 42).

[2] Empirical conditions in terms of psychological, biological or neurological factors that refer to our human nature like lack of will power, lack of reflection, habits, conflicting emotions and so forth are also to be considered here (Suchanek, 2015, p. 43).

3.1 Values: Successful Leadership of Global Virtual Teams

This section will bring business ethical concepts concerning cooperation and trust into the field of GVT leadership. The ethical dimension of trust in GVTs will be reflected here, where trust will be established as a fundamental condition of successful interactions in general and concerning GVTs in particular (3.1.1). Furthermore, the business ethical concept of the (extended) golden rule and its do no harm dimension will be introduced as an investment in the conditions for social cooperation for mutual benefit (Suchanek, 2015, p. 188). The core condition to invest in is trust, and the do no harm dimension can support this investment (3.1.2). Finally, this section introduces the ethical focal point do (illegitimate) harm (3.1.3). After analyzing what an ethical focal point is, it will be shown that do no illegitame harm can serve as common ground for trust in GVTs.

3.1.1 Trust as Fundamental Condition for Successful Interactions in Global Virtual Teams

This dissertation focuses on *interpersonal trust,* defined as the confidence in another person (or between two persons) and a willingness to be vulnerable to them or each other (Ma et al., 2019, p. 1).[3] There will be no further reference to this topic.

Trust has recently gained popularity within the academic and public realm in the last decades. Thanks to new business models of the sharing economy like Uber, Airbnb, and many others, the prominence and value of trust are steadily increasing (De Biasi, 2019). However, trust has also been brought into relation to an increased number of corporate crises and political scandals (Suchanek & von Broock, 2009). In light of the ongoing COVID-19 pandemic, trust has gained further attention, and a myriad of research has emerged (Kniffin et al., 2021; Wang et al., 2021). Generalized fear of the unknown and uncertainty about the end of the numerous lock down's travel restrictions, and vaccination obligations, heated discussions about the abolition of civil rights are further polarizing global societies, and have instilled a climate of mistrust concerning governments, banks, big corporations, the public health systems, amongst others. With regards to GVTs, trust has become an important topic, too. On the one hand, many leaders struggle with the effective leadership of remote workers. On the other hand, many remote

[3] This thesis deals with interpersonal trust in comparison to system-based trust.

employees feel untrusted and micromanaged by their leaders, resulting in less trust in their leader and the team. The consequences of poor virtual leadership have been proven to negatively impact the overall economy (Parker et al., 2020).

Regarding academic research on trust, although the topic of trust has been present for 50 years, there is still no consensus but rather a profound lack of agreement on a suitable definition of the concept (De Biasi, 2019, p. 88). Especially in the last 20 years, extensive quantitative and qualitative research has been conducted on trust in organizations (De Biasi, 2019; Ma et al., 2019). Due to the immensity of the research domain, many studies have focused on particular realms of trust, such as dyadic trust (Korsgaard et al., 2015), trust repair (Lewicki & Brinsfield, 2017), trust in leaders (Burke et al., 2007), trust across levels of an organization (Fulmer & Gelfand, 2012), as well as particular relationships between trust and outcomes, including individual performance (Colquitt et al., 2007), team performance (De Jong et al., 2016). With regards to teams and trust, the volume of published studies accelerated from less than ten before 2000 to over 100 by 2015 (De Jong, Dirks, & Gillespie, 2016), especially concerning interpersonal trust (Balliet & Van Lange, 2013; Ma et al., 2019) and trust in VTs (Breuer et al., 2016; Calefato & Lanubile, 2018; Cheng et al., 2016; Crisp & Jarvenpaa, 2013; Ford et al., 2017; Kanawattanachai & Yoo, 2002; Kayworth & Leidner, 2002). Even though researchers from various academic disciplines agree that trust is of the utmost importance in the conduct of human affairs (Hosmer, 1995, p. 379), due to the richness of meanings, trust remains a diffuse topic (De Biasi, 2019, p. 88).

The renowned social psychologist Morton Deutsch (1958) was a pioneer in the conceptualization of trust on which later research (Mayer et al., 1995; Rousseau et al., 1998) built its premise (De Biasi, 2019; Suurendonk, 2017). Deutsch recognized the importance of trust and related other concepts to its interpretation, such as suspicion, betrayal, and faith, to the understanding of social life and personality development, while realizing that trust further bears the notion of *expectation* or *predictability* (De Biasi, 2019; Deutsch, 1958). Other researchers added that trusting involves potential doubt (Lewis & Weigert, 1985) and taking a risk in an interpersonal encounter (Gunnthorsdottir et al., 2002). Thus, trusting includes the unavoidable element of risk, which needs to be accepted when granting trust to another individual. This risk is entailed in the fact that the trustor[4] will be worse off trusting and having the trust granted abused than not trusting at all (De Biasi, 2019, p. 88).

[4] The trustor is the person granting trust.

Moreover, in interpersonal trust situations, the trustee has the power to cause *harm* to the trustor by abusing the trust being granted. Suspicion emerges if the trustor is not certain about the trustee's[5] behavior. If both parties are aware of each other's intentions and are, in some ways, sure about the other's behavior and what to expect, the trustor and the trustee are said to have mutual trust (De Biasi, 2019). Further consensus concerning this definition of trust relates to the fact that one other party needs to be willing to be *vulnerable* to the other party (person or a group) (Mayer et al., 1995). Building on that, one of the most cited definitions of trust, which is equally used in the field of VT research, stems from Mayer et al. (1995). Trust is thus defined as "the willingness of a party to be vulnerable to the actions of another party based on the expectation that the other will perform a particular action important to the trustor irrespective of the ability to monitor or control that other party." (Mayer et al., 1995, p. 712). The authors' model proposes that trust is a function of the trustee's trustworthiness with regards to their (a) benevolence, which is about being supportive and caring; their (b) ability, which is about being competent and capable; and their (c) integrity, which is about being consistent and honest and the trustor's propensity to trust (Mayer et al., 1995). Additionally, in their integrative review of trust literature, Rousseau et al. (1998) underpin that trust is a "psychological state comprising the intention to accept vulnerability based upon positive expectations of the intentions or behavior of another" (Rousseau et al., 1998, p. 395).

According to Suchanek, this specificity of trust of being vulnerable to others' actions represents *the* most fundamental problem for human cooperation (2015, pp. 64, 72). This problem is further illustrated in the prisoners' dilemma, where two parties are supposed to decide to cooperate to achieve optimal turnout. Two major questions arise that ought to be answered (Suchanek, 2015, pp. 64–67):

(1) Can I trust the other to cooperate?
(2) How can I assure the other that I am going to cooperate?

The two parties involved are the trustor, the person trusting the other, and the trustee, the person honoring or abusing the trust. Consequently, the trustor is vulnerable and dependent on the trustee's actions. The trustee thereby gains power and/or control. Doing so gives the trustor certain expectations that justify or rationalize the decision-to-trust (De Biasi, 2019). Thus, to increase the likeliness of a decision-to-trust, the trustee has to express their trustworthiness. Furthermore,

[5] The trustee is the person receiving trust.

the context in which the decision-to-trust takes place also influences that decision (Flores & Solomon, 1998). This follows the practical syllogism and the fact that the empirical conditions frame a situation (Homann, 2014). Subsequently, the result is not only a question of will or intentions but also a question of ability (De Biasi, 2019, p. 88; Suchanek, 2015, p. 67).

From a (business) ethical point of view, the general function of trust is to engender reciprocal beneficial cooperation. Thus, trust forms the basis of long-term social cooperation (Suchanek, 2015, p. 68). This premise finds resonance in GVTs literature that has shown that trust is linked to positive aspects of collaboration and performance (Breuer et al., 2016; Ford et al., 2017; Hacker et al., 2019; Jarvenpaa & Leidner, 1999; Jawadi, 2013; Kayworth & Leidner, 2000). In their extensive research on trust in GVTs, Hacker et al. (2019) categorized the function and consequences of trust into the categories of performance (relations between the group and the environmental context), member well-being (the development and maintenance of the group as a system), and member support (ways in which the individual is embedded within the group). Thus, trust has been positively related to the three mentioned areas. Trust has especially been point out to be essential in overcoming all challenges related to communication, technology, and culture in GVTs (Hacker et al., 2019).

Furthermore, trust has been further linked in a positive manner to learning effectiveness (Edwards & Sridhar, 2005), creative problem solving (Murthy et al., 2013), and especially individual member performance and team performance in GVTs (Breuer et al., 2016; Kanawattanachai & Yoo, 2002; Sarker et al., 2011). Most VT authors agree that trust is crucial for all aspects of collaboration and is further positively linked to greater team cohesion and less turnover in GVTs (Breuer et al., 2016). Furthermore, trust reduces transaction costs (Suchanek, 2015). This applies, firstly, to the costs which would have otherwise occurred to protect oneself from opportunistic behavior from others (Suchanek, 2015). With regards to virtual collaboration, these costs refer to a limited flow of information within the team which can be detrimental to team performance and heighten transaction costs (Jarvenpaa & Leidner, 1999). Trust is essential for team effectiveness as it determines if team members will ask each other for support, share feedback, and discuss ticklish topics and disagreements (Breuer et al., 2016).

Moreover, trust reduces contingency and thus uncertainty. Contingency refers to the fact that reality may unfold in any number of (unexpected) ways, which resumes in uncertainty (Suchanek, 2015, p. 68). Trust reduces the number of potential, unknown outcomes, which is particularly important within the context of GVTs where team members work mostly alone and isolated with reduced interaction possibilities (Fajen, 2018; Jarvenpaa & Leidner, 1999). Trust is thus essential since virtual interactions lack contextual cues such as facial expressions and the tone of voice, making the intentions of others less visible (Breuer et al., 2016; Hacker et al., 2019). Trust is essential in GVTs to overcome technological difficulties that can create uncertainties within the team (Hacker et al., 2019). CMC media can fail and, consequently, lead to communication disruptions. GVTs with high team trust can give their co-workers the benefit of doubt when technology fails without falling into assumptions that could lead to conflicts (Hacker et al., 2019; Morrison-Smith & Ruiz, 2020). This is why many GVT researchers consider building mutual trust of the utmost importance in virtual collaboration (Fajen, 2018; Ford et al., 2017; Hacker et al., 2019).

In line with that, trust also reduces complexity as the behavior of others can be better predicted (Suchanek, 2015, p. 68). Thus, trust allows each party to disregard potential backup plans, alternatives, and control mechanisms, allowing for better cooperation. This goes hand in hand with the fact that trust increases flexibility. Especially in GVTs, members must constantly adjust to the fast-paced and uncertain environment while working with diverse socio-cultural team members (Fajen, 2018). Thus, GVT members need high self-leadership and self-responsibility. If members are trusted and can trust each other, there is no need for control and readjustments from GVL or other members. GVT members can resolve issues such as process delays without interference from GVL or others (Breuer et al., 2016; Hacker et al., 2019).

Finally, trust can motivate or encourage a cooperative disposition (Suchanek, 2015, p. 68). If individuals are trusted, they are more inclined to honor this trust and engage in trusting relationships. Individuals are furthermore inclined to accept the decisions of people they trust. In line with GVT research, socio-emotional processes such as trust, contentment, and commitment are linked and influence each other in virtual collaboration (Fajen, 2018, pp. 103–111, 301–305). Thus, trust in GVTs enhances individual commitment to the team and the project and enhances team member satisfaction (DeRosa et al., 2004; Morrison-Smith & Ruiz, 2020).

In sum, this subsection 3.1.1 has shown that trust is a fundamental condition for successful interactions in GVTs. It has been demonstrated that trust is an asset to ensure social cooperation for mutual benefit in GVTs. If it is present, it can generate returns regarding higher team performance, effectiveness, and member well-being which otherwise would not have been realizable (Suchanek, 2015, p. 63).

The following subchapter 3.1.2 will further underpin the importance of trust and introduce the (extended) golden rule and its do no harm dimension as the main condition to invest into for trust and long-term social cooperation for mutual benefit.

3.1.2 The Extended Golden Rule and its Do No harm Dimension

This subsection introduces the business ethical concept of the (extended) golden rule, and its implicit do no harm dimension. The contribution of this subsection is to recognize the advantage of do no harm as a morally accepted global standard that can be translated to all cultural contexts and can thus have the potential to act as a moral foundation for cooperation in diverse socio-cultural GVTs.

The golden rule defined in one version as "do not do what you do not want to be done to yourself," and its implicit do no harm dimension resonates with all religious and philosophical renditions and is accepted as a general moral standard (Neusner & Chilton, 2008; Singer, 1963). As a cross-cultural ethical precept, also known as the "Ethic of Reciprocity" (Neusner & Chilton, 2008), it can be rendered in either positive or negative formulations and has thus been defined in a multitude of ways within respective cultural contexts:

Christianity: In everything, do to others as you would have them do to you, for this is the law of the prophets (Jesus, Matthew 7:12).

Zoroastrianism: Do not do unto others whatever is injurious to yourself (Shayaste-na Shayast 13.29).

Judaism: What is hateful to you, do not do to your neighbor; this is the whole Torah; all the rest is commentary (Hillel, Talmud, Shabbat 31a).

Islam: Not one truly believes until you wish for others what you want (The Prophet Muhammed, Hadith).

Buddhism: Treat not others in ways that you would fund hurtful (Udana-Varga 5.18).

Thus, as a fundamental universal ethical norm, the do no harm principle guides human behavior across cultures, religions, disciplines, times, and contexts and can be found in various contexts and even in formal law systems (Singer, 1963). Article 4 of the Declaration of Rights of Man and of Citizen, passed by France's National Constituent Assembly in August 1789, includes references to the golden rule: "La liberté consiste à pouvoir faire tout ce qui ne nuit pas à autrui." "which translates into English as: "Freedom consists in being able to do everything that does not harm others." (Legifrance, 2022).

Moreover, the do no harm principle also finds resonance in management literature. According to renowned management scholar Peter F. Drucker, an effective leader should avoid harm: "The first responsibility of a professional [is …] primum non nocere—Above all, not knowingly to do harm." (Drucker, 1986, pp. 256–257). Drucker refers to the fact that any professional, be it a lawyer or doctor, should try not to do harm even though nobody can guarantee that no harm will occur. Regarding leaders, they often do want to realize do no harm. However, they cannot avoid harm given the empirical conditions for actions they are embedded in. Moreover, according to the Wittenberg Centre for Global Ethics, the do no harm principle is relevant for (virtual) teamwork and cooperation as this principle is fundamental for long-term social cooperation (WCGE, 2017, p. 3).

However, according to Wattles, the different formulations of doing no harm also have other implications. They are embedded in different (socio-cultural) contexts, which raises the question of whether the same concept is at work or not (Wattles, 1996, p. 4). Wattles states that "the meaning of the golden rule depends on its context and language and culture are not reliable clues for identifying conceptual similarity and differences." (Wattles, 1996, p. 4). Thus, for some, the golden rule functions as an authoritative approach; for others, it refers to general tradition or personal commitment. Subsequently, the golden rule consists for some of one rule and for others of several rules. The golden rule can be interpreted in a religious context or have no religious association at all (Wattles, 1996, p. 4). The point is that the meaning of the golden rule is by no standard the same in different cultural contexts, which also implies that the concept of harm varies (Wattles, 1996, p. 5).

Generally speaking, the golden rule provides a universally comprehensible tool for handling conflictual situations. The do no harm principle implies the guiding idea that the impact of an individual's use of freedom should principally not harm others or violate their legitimate expectations (Suchanek, 2008). Thus, do no harm is a twofold concept that refers to both actions and expectations. On the one hand, this principle provides orientation for individuals to answer what one should (not) reasonably do, at least without giving a good reason. On the other hand, the golden rule helps to set reasonable expectations of other individuals with whom one interacts or who is affected regarding one's own use of freedom (Suchanek, 2007, 2008). Subsequently, people do not want to be harmed, and the reciprocal expectation is that humans should not harm other humans.

Suchanek (2007) introduces the (extended) golden rule within an economical and business ethics context as "Invest in the conditions of social cooperation for mutual benefit!" (p. 38). The (extended) golden rule contains the following four orientations (Suchanek, 2015, p. 188):

A) The orientation on *investment*
B) The orientation on *mutual advantage*
C) The orientation on *generalizability* (social cooperation)
D) The orientation on *conditions*

1) The orientation of *investment* refers to the abstinence from short-term advantages as an investment in the longer-term goals. Moral actions are often associated with the abstinence from something whereby one's own interests are put aside. Suchanek translates this idea into the economic term of *investment* to motivate people in the conception of business ethics (Suchanek, 2015, p. 188). Investment refers to abstaining from harming others through self-binding measures for achieving beneficial long-term results. Thus, investment underpins the consequences of actions and future outcomes.
2) The idea of *reciprocity* is represented in *mutual advantage* (Suchanek, 2015, p. 188). In line with Immanuel Kant's argument for the moral importance of recognizing every individual as an "end in themselves," the idea of mutual advantage acknowledges and respects the advantage of not only oneself but of others; first and foremost, by not causing them illegitimate harm, which will be further elaborated on in 3.1.3.
3) With regards to the orientation on generalizability, the (extended) golden rule aims at *social cooperation* (Suchanek, 2015, p. 188). This idea includes not only all stakeholders directly affected by an action but also future generations. Respecting others means thus not harming third parties.
4) This last point of orientation refers to the (supportive) conditions for social cooperation (Suchanek, 2015, p. 188). These conditions include those that are advantageous to successful social cooperation, such as human capital—in terms of virtue but competencies necessary for cooperation for mutual advantage, social and institutional capital, and especially trust (Suchanek, 2007, p. 51). *Trust is* the essential condition to invest in for social cooperation.

Overall, the (extended) golden rule overcomes the classical conflict between morality and self-interest from a philosophical perspective by introducing enlightened self-interest without rejecting the claim of morality (Suchanek, 2007, p. 20). As it is based on reciprocity, the intention of the (extended) golden rule is to improve social cooperation on all sides of collaboration. The general distrust in pursuing self-interest stems from a Kantian-based philosophy and resulted in concepts of ethics where an act of morality must come from obligation and not from inclination (Suchanek, 2008, p. 3). Within the realm of Economic ethics, however, humans are recognized as empirical beings subject to all kinds of empirical conditions (i.e., biological, psychological, social, etc.). They can thus not always act against their own self-interest, especially not in the long term. Individuals are seen as moral subjects who possess dignity, are endowed with freedom, and can thus act freely. It follows that (individual) freedom only exists within a particular situation's limits and boundaries (Suchanek, 2008, p. 2). Morality applied to individuals must therefore be compatible with their respective self-interest in given situations. The (extended) golden rule highlights the importance of implementabilty and embeddedness in reality. Therefore, only enlightened self-interest, directed at mutual benefits, including those of other stakeholders involved, and avoiding harm (also to members of society who are not part of the team), is morally acceptable (Suchanek, 2008, p. 3). The critical factor in bridging the divide between morality and self-interest is the responsible use of own's freedom, which implies self-binding measures and some costs for the individual. Therefore, investing in one's future freedom is of the utmost importance to fulfilling the (extended) golden rule's purpose of fostering long-term social cooperation for mutual benefit (Suchanek, 2008, p. 5).

Applied to GVL to be able to avoid harm (in challenging situations) and thus invest in the conditions of social cooperation for mutual benefit, leaders need the power of moral judgment and competencies to design the conditions of actions for their followers (and team members) to act accordingly (Suchanek, 2015, p. 164). In line with prior VT research, the leader-followership relationship plays a crucial role in building and sustaining trust in GVTs (Fajen, 2018; Ford et al., 2017; Jawadi, 2013). GVL is thus required to act as a role model for their team members to follow (cf. 2.3.3, 3.3.3, 3.3.4). Additionally, given the lack of frequent face-to-face interactions or informal communication, GVL needs to have specific skills and character traits to compensate (cf. 2.3.2). GVL needs to respond to task-related roles and socio-emotional needs of its members while accommodating the spatial, structural and cultural dispersion reflected in linguistic, work style, experimental and other cultural differences (Ford et al., 2017, p. 4). GVL should invest in trust by acquiring these specific skills and be adequately trained in delegation, goal setting, role clarification, conflict resolution, and self-management. (Ford et al., 2017, p. 4). Acquiring these skills are additional costs in terms of money, time, and effort which demands GVL to cut down their resources from other projects.

Moreover, GVL can invest in trust by acquiring intercultural competencies. As harm is always embedded within a specific context, GVL should be aware that the notion of harm can have specific and different meanings and implications concerning different socio-cultural contexts of team members (3.2.1, 3.2.2). GVL should thus invest in acquiring intercultural competencies and be trained in cultural awareness to properly analyze and interpret the potential conflictual situation to respond adequately (Ford et al. 2017). This difference in the meaning of harm in GVTs will be further elucidated in 3.2.1 and 3.2.2 regarding differences in trust expectations in GVT and the importance of creating a shared understanding of do no (illegitimate) harm.

Furthermore, GVL can invest in trust and avoid harm by adequately selecting and preparing GVT members as team composition plays a crucial role in trust-building (Ford et al., 2017, p. 4). GVL should be aware that some people can work in virtual settings better than others. There are essential personality characteristics and personal values that influence team success, such as a willingness to trust, a positive view of the organization and its mission, the skill of self-management, and an ability to communicate and cooperate with others in a virtual work environment (Clark et al., 2010). This means that GVL should take enough time (which bears costs) to select GVT members to realize do no harm and thus invest in the future benefits of social cooperation.

Regarding practicality, shorter versions of the golden rule can serve as heuristic and orient GVL in how to deal with GVT members in general. GVL can follow the premise of "*put yourself in the other person's shoes!*" which represents a common version of the golden rule found in everyday language use. This version of the rule is beneficial in a trust relationship. This will be shown based on the real-life example of the company Think-it and show how GVL could manage to give and receive constructive feedback, as laid out in detail in *3.3. Investment* and *3.4. Case Illustration.* The case has stated that it highly matters how feedback is given for it to be well received. The version mentioned above of the golden rule allows GVL to take a moment to put themselves in the shoes of the employee or team member who will receive the feedback. This exercise may not affect the concrete details of the situation, but it may change how the action is carried out and received (Suchanek, 2015). This is not only helpful for the affected team member to better deal with the situation and to spur the learning curve, but also a signal to others about how they can expect to be dealt with in other interactions and sensitive situations, i.e., it can be an investment in trust in GVTs. Thus, GVL should at least signal and act in a way that respects the do no harm principle.

This example raises another critical question: Is, do no harm possible or realistic in GVT contexts? In business ethics, the pressure of competition constraints can lead to the externalization of costs (Suchanek, 2017). With regards to GVTs, this means that given the fact that these teams work in a fast-paced context, driven by agility, self-reliance, and information asymmetries, chances are high that some harm will happen, undermining trust and trust expectations of team members. The point here is that the do no harm principle can sometimes be impossible to follow due to empirical constraints and a difference in understanding of what harm means. Due to socio-cultural differences, the notion of harm can differ significantly in GVTs. A minimum consent has to be elaborated towards a shared understanding of harm and, more specifically, of do no (illegitimate) harm. Some forms of harm can, under certain circumstances, have legitimacy. This discussion leads to the following subsection on the (il-)legitimacy of harm, which is fundamental for good teamwork and cooperation.

3.1.3 The Ethical Focal Point Do No Illegitimate Harm as Common Ground in Global Virtual Teams

This subsection will further elaborate on the do no harm principle and merge the business ethical concept of the ethical focal point "do no illegitimate harm" and the concept of common ground, which has been deemed as of the utmost importance for trust in GVTs. The point of this section is that the ethical focal point do no (illegitimate) harm can serve as common ground in GVTs if it is a shared understanding, thus enabling trust and enhancing performance.

First, focal points were introduced as a solution to pure coordination games with two players in a conflictual situation who are unable to communicate but want to coordinate their actions for mutual advantage (Schelling, 1980). Focal points are, therefore, elements of "each person's expectation of what the other expects him to expect to be expected to do" (Schelling, 1980, p. 57). Focal points help to coordinate expectations about the other player's potential actions and align their actions accordingly (Suchanek & Entschew, 2018). From a game's theoretical perspective, a focal point needs to be *common knowledge* to function as a focal point (Kreps, 1990). Subsequently, both players need to know that the other player is equally aware that there is a focal point in place that coordinates their (inter-)actions, thus enabling effective cooperation.

With regards to GVTs, explicit communication is lacking and potentially hindering effective teamwork and performance (cf. 2.2.2, cf. 2.2.3); focal points can guide behavior and expectations. A common example in GVTs concerns time management and the respective "team working hours window" This is particularly tricky when team members are globally dispersed and work in different time zones (Treinen & Miller-Frost, 2006). To coordinate GVTs GVL needs to create a proper work schedule for its team. For example, GVL defines the respective working hours as eight hours in each country without giving a specific time frame to individual team members. In this case, the focal point is the eight-hour working window with GVT members clocking their time in their project management intranet, allowing all GVT members to be aware when who is working online. This point of intersection is the basic principle of shared behavioral expectations as a primary condition for successful cooperation (Suchanek & Entschew, 2018, p. 224).

Moreover, focal points can also enable cooperation by coordinating actions in a dynamic game and are fundamental principles that can be used to effectively deal with "unforeseen contingencies" (Kreps, 1990, p. 92). Characterized by types of conflicts that are not (sufficiently) regulated through formal or informal rules, these unforeseen contingencies can harm cooperation (Bowles, 2016). Focal points can establish a shared understanding of how to deal in such a situation between both transacting parties (Kreps, 1990). Thus, if such an unforeseen contingency arises, cooperating partners may need to trust that the other party will not use the opportunity to realize benefits at the contracting party's expense. Thus, focal points could help in these situations.

Especially in GVTs, many unforeseen contingencies can arise due to their spatial, temporal, and structural dispersion and other dimensions of virtuality (cf. 2.1.3) while being embedded in the VUCA[6] world. Dynamic changes in (social) expectations and conditions for action can occur regularly, thus undermining effective cooperation (Suchanek & Entschew, 2018). This holds particularly true for GVTs and their challenges for effective cooperation related to communication, the use of technology, and socio-cultural differences (cf. 2.2.2) that have been shown to have detrimental effects on long-term social cooperation and performance (cf. 2.2.3) and trust (cf. 2.2.3). Coming back to the GVTs' example of scheduling appropriate work hours, even though work hours have been fixed for example at eight hours per day, some team members may bend this rule due to matters of urgency (3.2.1).[7] The sense of urgency is one of the cultural dimensions alongside which one can measure differences in understanding, behavior, and expectations between different cultures (Hofstede, 1984, 1993). People's sense of urgency differs dramatically regarding their socio-cultural background and prior experiences. For instance, team member A may bend the rule

[6] Acronym for volatile, uncertain, complex, ambiguous.

[7] This point will be further elaborated on in cf. 3.2.1.

of eight hours per day and (over)work concerning a specific project they may see as urgent to accomplish, thus working longer than the recommended hours.

Furthermore, this team member's child may be sick (unforeseen contingency). Therefore, they may feel compelled to get all the work done to care for the child as soon as possible. Team member A may solicit other team members (B and C) to equally work on the project (which often is the case in GVTs due to the interdependency of tasks). However, these team members may not share the same sense of urgency and do not encounter the same personal issues, thus being unwilling to continue working on that specific project. Their eight-hour working window has already passed, which is visible on the log-in system of the organization. The consequence is that the focal point of the "team working hours window of eight hours" fails to function concerning aligning expectations and coordinating actions. This situation can create animosities and conflict between these team members and in the team in general, especially if one does not know about the personal issues of team member A. Team members B and C may feel their privacy as eing invaded and further feel disrespected by team member A. This situation leaves room for all kinds of assumptions and biases from all parties that could lead to conflict and mistrust.

This example shows that focal points may fail to fulfill their function of aligning expectations in GVTs due to a lack of shared understanding concerning the focal principle. As focal points are essential elements of the order of communication, a *shared understanding* of the focal point and its implication in specific situations is imperative to fulfilling its function (Suchanek & Entschew, 2018, p. 224). Focal points must be enriched with meaning to become properly applicable in concrete situations (Kreps, 1990, pp. 127–129) and be further embedded in formal and informal norms (Suchanek & Entschew, 2018). Leaders can use normative points of orientation to define shared goals, values, and interests and empirical points of orientation such as rules for the concretization and coordination of actions (Suchanek, 2015, pp. 142–143). Rules are of the utmost importance as they engender mutual behavioral reliability and allow social cooperation, especially regarding conflict situations (Suchanek, 2015, p. 148).

Moreover, leaders should lead by example, following the focal principle to further demonstrate its importance in the team (Suchanek, 2019)(3.2.3, 3.3.4). Furthermore, focal points can still align expectations and coordinate actions despite conflicting perceptions of the situation, thanks to shared team experience over time (Kreps, 1990). Focal points are, thus, in part, the product of experience, which can be taught through repeated application (Kreps, 1990, pp. 122–123).

Especially concerning GVTs, shared work experience makes virtual cooperation easier, but it takes more time to establish common conceptual frameworks (Cundill, Harvey, Tebboth, Cochrane, Currie-Alder, et al., 2019).

Moreover, Suchanek and Entschew (2018) introduce *ethical* focal points as "oral principles, standards, or values that form the basis of consistent normative expectations and that can "provide an orientation of what to *reasonably* expect others to do and correspondingly what one should *reasonably* take into consideration in one's own actions in order to realize gains from social cooperation and avoid undue harm" (Suchanek & Entschew, 2018, p. 225). Moreover, the authors introduce the *do no harm* as the prime example of an ethical focal point (2018, p. 229, authors' emphasis) and argue: "Ethical focal points can be seen as an answer to the question, *what can we reasonably expect from each other?* The most basic answer to this question is, in our opinion, given by the principle *do no harm.*"

This point is of the utmost importance for this dissertation; the expectation of not being harmed is the most basic trust expectation referring to the vulnerability of respective stakeholders (Suchanek, 2015, pp. 64–121).[8] However, it is essential to specify the do no harm principle with the concept of legitimacy. Under certain conditions for action, the expectation to avoid all harm, in any case, is *impossible to fulfill* (Suchanek, 2019). Avoiding harm can imply costs or burdens for oneself and/or others (Suchanek & Entschew, 2018). According to Suchman, "l]egitimacy is a generalized perception or assumption that the actions of an entity are desirable, proper, or appropriate within some socially constructed system of norms, values, beliefs, and definitions." (Suchman, 1995, p. 574). Moreover, legitimacy can be understood "as the generalized authority or social acceptability to act in a way which implies some potential or actual burden (costs, risks, harm) on others for justifiable reasons. "(Suchanek, 2019, p. 6). This refers to the fact that one should at least have a *legitimate* reason when harming others.

According to Suchanek, this notion of legitimacy is grounded in "(societal) consent, including ways to maintain or create consent in dissent" (Suchanek, 2019, p. 15). Referring to the *appropriateness* of harm, formal systems of law and regulations and informal institutions such as moral and cultural rules, norms, and routines can help define and discern forms of harm concerning the legitimacy and the scope of harm (Suchanek & Entschew, 2018). Thus, (ethical) focal points should have the following four qualities to fulfill their functioning and act as a "token of trust": first, they should "be (sufficiently) *consistent* with other perceptions, like universally accepted principles, norms, values or generally

[8] This point will find further explanation in 3.2.1.

recognized facts and patters about reality, second, they should be *understandable* and resonate with ordinary people, third they should be *stable* and remain their meaning over time and finally, finally, they should be *self-enforcing* through embedment in routines while being incentive-compatible (Suchanek & Entschew, 2018, pp. 224–227).

Moreover, to function as an ethical focal point for trust, harm's (il-)legitimacy needs a sufficiently shared understanding of its meaning in specific situations (Suchanek & Entschew, 2018, p. 224). Especially in GVTs, the notion of (illegitimate) harm differs due to socio-cultural backgrounds that highly influence the meaning and interpretations of concepts and situations (cf. 3.2.1). Thus, to align trust expectations and actions, the ethical focal point do no (illegitimate) harm has to become a shared understanding between all GVT members to be useful to coordinate (trust) expectations and actions. Thus, as a focal principle, it needs to be enriched with meaning to become properly applicable in concrete situations (Kreps, 1990, pp. 127–129).

This importance of a shared understanding regarding communication has been highlighted by VT research and further referred to as common ground (Cundill et al., 2019; G. M. Olson & Olson, 2000; J. Olson & Olson, 2011). In GVTs effective communication as the basis for cooperation between people requires that the communicative exchange occurs concerning some level of *common ground* (Clark, 1996; Olson & Olson, 2000). Similarly to Kreps' (1990) premise of *common knowledge* with regards to focal points, *common ground* refers to that knowledge that the participants or members have in common and about which they are aware they have it in common (Clark, 1996).

(Virtual) Collaboration is more effective if team members have *common ground* (H. Clark, 1996; H. H. Clark & Brennan, 1991; Cundill et al., 2019; Maynard & Gilson, 2014; G. M. Olson & Olson, 2000; J. Olson & Olson, 2011). This includes, amongst others, a shared 'community of practice' (Cundill, Harvey, Tebboth, Cochrane, Currie-Alder, et al., 2019), shared experience, vocabulary, and communication (Olson & Olson, 2011, p. 1) or a shared (team) mental model (SMM) (Maynard & Gilson, 2014). Regarding SMMs, they are one of the main topics of this dissertation and will be further elaborated on in 3.2.2.

While a solid foundation of common ground is highly beneficial for team effectiveness and cooperation in GVTs, the lack of it can lead to conflict and disruption (Olson & Olson, 2000, p. 148). Lack of common ground results in miscommunication and misinterpretation of information, thus hindering effective collaboration (Cramton, 2001). The consequence of a lack of common ground resumes in challenges concerning building trust in GVTs (Jarvenpaa & Leidner, 1999; Zolin et al., 2004). Thus, establishing common ground is of the utmost importance in GVTs for their well-functioning and performance (Morrison-Smith & Ruiz, 2020, p. 16).

Regarding the ethical focal point, do no (illegitimate) harm, which coordinates respective (trust) expectations and actions; it is significant in GVTs for a two-fold reason. First, it can serve as common ground in GVTs regarding a community of practice elaborated on by VT research as of the utmost importance for trust. Second, it can align trust expectations and actions if it is a shared understanding between all team members. Thus, the ethical focal point do no (illegitimate harm) is a fundamental condition for trust and, therefore, effective cooperation and performance in GVTs.

The following section will elaborate on the reality of trust-building in GVTs concerning the formation of trust expectations (3.2.1), the role of a shared (team) mental model concerning the illegitimacy of harm for trust (3.2.2), and the importance of GVL to role model trustworthy behavior in GVTs (3.2.3).

3.2 Reality: How Different Trust Expectations and Leadership Influence Trust in Global Virtual Teams

This section deals with the empirical realities concerning trust-building in GVTs. Section 3.2 represents the 2nd order of the business ethical heuristical tool of the practical syllogism and refers to the question (2) "*What can I/we do?*". This question relates to the multitude of empirical obstacles and constraints, including money, resources, time, market competition, and so forth, interfering with the realization of (1) values, intentions, and goals (Suchanek, 2015, p. 43). To stay in the scope of this thesis research, section 3.2 elaborates specifically on the challenges to trust-building that GVL can overcome regarding the formation of respective trust expectations in GVTs related to the impact of socio-cultural differences (3.2.1). Further, this section will underpin the importance of an SMM of the illegitimacy of harm for trust in GVTs. Finally, this section will elaborate on the importance of explicit GVL for trust and underpin GVL's function to role-model trustworthiness in GVTs. Other challenges and aspects of trust-building are not the scope of this dissertation and will not be further elucidated or referred to. While all subsections of this section elaborate on the challenges mentioned above regarding trust-building in GVTs, they offer the solution to how to overcome the given barrier. These answers to the challenges will be further summarized and combined in 3.3, which answers the research question.

3.2.1 Different Trust Expectations in Global Virtual Teams

This subsection builds on the last subsection's (cf. 3.1.1) point that has shown that the ethical focal point do no (illegitimate) harm is a fundamental condition for trust in teams and thus for effective cooperation and performance in GVTs useful to serve as common ground. This subsection will elaborate on the formation of trust relationships and respective trust expectations influenced by different socio-cultural backgrounds. The point of this subsection is to underpin further the importance of a shared understanding regarding the ethical focal point do no (illegitimate) harm in GVTs to form mutual reliable trust expectations and actions.

First, with regards to the trust relationship, the trust game can offer insights. It involves two interacting parties, trustor A[9] and trustee[10] B (Kreps, 1990, p. 100; Suchanek, 2015, pp. 69–71):

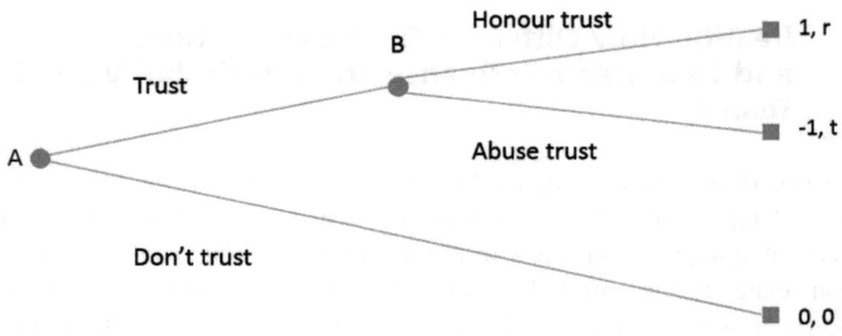

The trust game (Suchanek, 2015, p. 70)

These two players are in a situation of possible cooperation. Trustor A can either grant or not grant trust to trustee B. If A chooses to trust, it is B's turn to either honor or abuse the trust vested by A. Either option results in a payoff for B. If B honors A's trust, A gets a payoff of 1, and B receives a payoff of r. If B abuses A's trust, A receives a payoff of −1, and B gets a payoff of t. If A, however, decides not to grant trust in the first place and hence forecloses B's decision whether to honor or abuse trust, both end up with a payoff of 0. The aim is for both to cooperate to realize mutual benefits (De Biasi, 2019, pp. 82–86).

[9] The term *trustor* refers to the person that decides to grant or not trust.

[10] The term *trustee* refers to the person to whom trust is granted or not. This person has the power to decide whether or not to honor the granted trust.

The trust relationship entails the two related yet distinct concepts of trusting and trustworthiness (Ben-Ner & Halldorsson, 2010). As illustrated in the trust game, this trust relationship manifests the two fundamental problems of trust translated into the following questions that ought to be answered by the trustor and the trustee (Suchanek, 2015, p. 65).[11]

(1) First, with regards to the problem of trusting, the question arises: How will the trustee, with whom the trustor (has to) interact(s), use her freedom (in the future) or, put in simple words, can A trust B to cooperate?
(2) Second, regarding the trustworthiness problem, the question arises: How can the trustee credibly signal her trustworthiness (to win the trustor for cooperation) or, simply, how can B convince A to cooperate?[12] (Suchanek, 2015, p. 65).[13]

The central issues characterizing the relationship between the trustor and the trustee are *vulnerability* and *insecurity* (Suchanek, 2015, pp. 71–73). According to Gambetta, trust is also related to the fact that agents have a degree of freedom to disappoint others' expectations (Gambetta, 1988, p. 218). Vulnerability results from the trustee's (B) freedom of choice and the situational conflict they might face (Suchanek, 2015, p. 83). A situational conflict might arise through empirical conditions framing the situation, which can be related to non-constructive incentives that incite the trustee (B) to abuse the trustor's (A) trust or missing abilities that keep the trustee from honoring the trustor's trust. This shows that cooperation is a question of the trustee's will or presumably (good) intentions as well as her abilities (Flores & Solomon, 1998, p. 221; Suchanek, 2015, p. 70). In a situational conflict, the trustee can *exploit the trustor's vulnerability* to gain (at least short-term) advantages at the trustor's expense (Suchanek, 2015, p. 84).[14] By deciding to abuse the trustor's trust, the trustee may do so at the cost of the trustor's future cooperativeness.[15] The trustor may be well aware of the trustee's situational conflict and will therefore consider whether or not to trust and cooperate depending

[11] The obvious aim is to cooperate and thus to gain maximum output for trustor and trustee.
[12] In the context of GVTs this translate into how can GVT members and especially GVL signal trustworthiness in order to win GVT members for cooperation?
[13] In the context of GVTs this translates into how can GVT members trust each other and their leader?
[14] It is assumed that the value of not honoring trust is bigger than the value of honouring trust
[15] It is assumed that granting and honoring trust is the best option for both parties for long-term social cooperation.

on their expectations regarding how the trustee will use her freedom of choice (Suchanek, 2015, p. 71).

Another propensity of the trust relationship is insecurity (Suchanek, 2015, p. 74). In a trust situation, the trustor is unsure how the trustee will use his freedom. The trustor cannot know the precise details of the situation related to the payoffs the trustee faces, her true intention, or how she might perceive the situation (Suchanek, 2015, p. 74). The degree of uncertainty varies significantly and depends on the available information about the situation and the ability to interpret this information reasonably (De Biasi, 2019). Irrespective of the amount of effort put into determining rules and incentives; uncertainty will never be eliminated (Suchanek, 2015, p. 74). Uncertainty is always related to the fact that the trustee is free, which is why a 'leap of faith' is an unavoidable element of trusting (Nikolova et al., 2015).[16] This advanced act of trust has also been underpinned in GVT literature and referred to as 'swift trust,' which is naturally given in GVTs at the beginning of the cooperation but fragile and therefore needs to be further promoted and sustained to turn into long-standing trust (Crisp & Jarvenpaa, 2013).

Moreover, trust is a device for coping with the freedom of others (Gambetta, 1988, p. 219). Both the trustor and the trustee's freedom to enter the cooperation depends on their alternatives and the inherent opportunity costs that might influence their decision to cooperate (Suchanek, 2015, p. 75). This shows that granting and honoring trust is an investment in the conditions for future cooperation to mutual advantage (Suchanek, 2015).[17] Thus, to deal with the freedom of others and in situations marked by vulnerability and insecurity, focal points, especially the ethical focal point, do no (illegitimate) harm for trust, can serve as orientation and align respective trust expectations and actions to further effective cooperation (cf. 3.1.1).

Furthermore, the trust relationship between trustor and trustee entails trust expectations (Suchanek, 2015, pp. 64–121). The trustor has certain (normative) expectations, which result from his evaluation of (1) the situation, i.e., the empirical conditions of action, as well as his assumptions about (2) how the trustee will deal with this situation, i.e., her (perceived) intentions and competences, which are a result of the information available on his reputation as well as the

[16] A leap of faith cannot be reduced to rational calculation or rules. It is always a question of the trustor's freedom (Suchanek, 2015, p. 75).

[17] Trust is thus only possible between two free actors and can never be forced (Suchanek, 2015, p. 75).

trustor's own experience in interacting with the trustee (Suchanek, 2015, pp. 70–80, 101). Some of the determinants influencing trust expectations refer to the general attitude of the trustor and his tendency to trust or to distrust, opportunism and non-opportunism, his risk aversion or affinity, as well as his stance on cooperation as win-win or win-lose interactions (Suchanek, 2015, pp. 81–82). Respectively, trust expectations are built on the trustee's trustworthiness, referring to the fact that she is not taking advantage of the trustor's vulnerability (Ben-Ner & Halldorsson, 2010) or not harming the legitimate trust expectations of the trustor (Suchanek, 2015, p. 88).

Trustworthiness is a general quality of the trustee characterized by competence (ability) and, most notably, by integrity (willingness) to self-commit in a situational conflict to respect the legitimate trust expectations of the trustor (Suchanek, 2015, pp. 87–88). Integrity is the key element of trustworthiness, and the general attitude of the trustee characterized by keeping promises, keeping rules and norms, and adhering to moral norms and values, especially concerning respect and fairness, among others (Suchanek, 2015, p. 88). Thus, demonstrating trustworthiness consistency regarding aligning words and actions regarding promises, rules, and moral values creates reliability for the trustor (Suchanek, 2015, p. 89). Thus, the ethical focal point do no (illegitimate) harm as a normative premise allows to form mutual trust expectations while coordinating the actions of both the trustor and the trustee by making their actions generally more predictable and aligned and, therefore, cooperation more likely to occur (Suchanek & Entschew, 2018). Since effective cooperation is the ultimate goal, it is worthwhile to invest in points of orientation for social cooperation for mutual advantage (Suchanek, 2015, p. 141), thus, it is worth investing in the ethical focal point do no (illegitimate) harm for trust.

Consequently, trust expectations are based on a *shared understanding of illegitimate harm* between all GVT members. A trustor's expectations are generally embedded in his understanding of the game[18] (Suchanek, 2015, pp. 39–41), which refers to his understanding and interpretation of (illegitimate) harm. Depending on their own understanding of the game, people may choose drastically different courses of action in a situation that is objectively the same (cf. 3.1.1). This 'understanding' refers to people's intentions, beliefs, and perceptions about how their intentions can be realized in a given situation (Suchanek, 2015,

[18] There are three levels of the game. The *understanding of the game* refers to the 1st level of the game; the two other levels refer to rules, and action (Suchanek, 2015, pp. 39–41).

p. 77).[19] Thus, how interacting parties perceive and interpret a given situation impacts their respective trust expectations.

As GVT members are, per definition, socio-culturally diverse, a shared understanding with regards to (the illegitimacy) of harm to form mutual legitimate trust expectations is naturally not given (cf. 3.1.3). As recognized by Kotlarsky and Oshri (2005), a culture profoundly impacts how people interpret and react in a given situation. More precisely, members of GVTs with different socio-cultural backgrounds are likely to have different behaviors within their team, including how they interact with their teammates (Jarvenpaa & Leidner, 1999).[20] Thus, different people give a different meaning to a situation based on their socio-cultural background and belonging (Agerfalk et al., 2005, p. 2). This is resumed regarding socio-cultural distance, a complex dimension involving national culture and language, organizational culture, politics, individual motivations, and work ethics (Dekker et al., 2008; Staples & Zhao, 2006) (cf. 2.1.1). It measures an actor's understanding of another actor's values and normative practices (Agerfalk et al., 2005, p. 4) (cf. 2.1.1). The cultural composition of GVTs has been recognized as the key predictor of a team's performance (Swigger et al., 2004). Prior GVT research has used Hofstede's cultural dimensions theory (Hofstede, 1984, 1993, 2011) to compare socio-cultural distance concerning the organizational context in (virtual) teams (Dekker et al., 2008; Staples & Zhao, 2006).[21] According to Swigger et al. (2004), cultural attributes are most strongly correlated to group performance, including attitudes about organizational hierarchy, harmony, trade-offs between future and current needs, and beliefs about how much influence individuals have on their fate (p. 365). Moreover, socio-cultural distance is associated with higher levels of conflict and lower levels of satisfaction and cohesion and thus

[19] It is assumed that the trustor is aware that the trustee has strengths and weaknesses as an empirical human being, who follows her own interests which may vary significantly. The trustor will generally not assume that the trustee will act against her own interests or incentives in the given situation. The question is how well the trustor knows and/or can judge the situational incentives and pay-offs. Disappointed expectations on behalf of the trustor may result from the fact that the trustor simply knows every little about the incentives and conflicts faced by the respective trustee (De Biasi, 2019; Suchanek, 2015, p. 77).

[20] Socio-cultural differences go beyond national differences. There are various subcultures within a nation and the national culture may not be entirely shared by all (B. Kirkman & Shapiro, 2005).

[21] The original theory proposes four dimensions alongside cultural values can be analysed: individualism-collectivism; uncertainty avoidance; power distance (strength of social hierarchy) and masculinity-femininity (task-orientation versus person-orientation). Later the dimensions of long-term orientation and the dimension of indulgence versus self-restraint were added and all dimensions were further deconstructed into sub domains.

profoundly impacts team performance in GVTs (Staples & Zhao, 2006, p. 392).[22] Delays and conflicts arise due to coordination and cooperation issues related to misunderstandings and differences regarding work practices and methodologies in GVTs (Staples & Zhao, 2006, p. 392).

The previously given example in cf. 3.1.1 with regards to *the sense of urgency* (to complete a specific project in this case) as part of Hofstede's framework differs dramatically concerning socio-cultural interpretations (cf. 3.1.1). One of the most prominent cultural dimensions in Hofstede's approach refers to the relative degree to which a particular culture is *formal* versus *informal* (Hofstede, 1984). Given the socio-culturally diverse composition of GVTs, they often consist of individuals from both formal and informal cultures. As a result, team members may have conflicting perspectives on certain attitudes related to project schedules, planning, and punctuality with deadlines (Kayworth & Leidner, 2000, p. 187), reflected in their *sense of urgency.* While more formal cultures like Asian cultures (Japan, Taiwan, Corea) tend to have a greater sense of urgency to set specific timetables and to diligently keep to deadlines, more informal cultures like Western cultures (USA, Anglo-Saxon, Germanic, and Scandinavian countries) may place less emphasis on setting and meeting deadlines as diligently. Saunders et al.'s analysis show how different cultural perceptions of time can give rise to tensions and impact team performance negatively (Saunders et al., 2004). Within the American, Anglo-Saxon, Germanic, and Scandinavian cultures, a clock time vision is dominant, where time is viewed as a scarce commodity drawing on a linear perception of time. In comparison, the Japanese perception of time views time as a cyclical, recurrent entity in unlimited supply (Saunders et al., 2004, p. 21). Along with this finding comes different expectations regarding how many hours a day team members are expected to work or differing definitions of what it means to work hard. With regards to our previous example about respective working hours in a GVT (cf. 3.1.3), GVT members from more formal countries like Japan may bend the rule on working hours and hence, could potentially do harm to other members from informal cultures like Germany, by putting co-workers into an uncomfortable position, that bears the potential for various misunderstandings, assumptions and conflicts thus negatively impacting team performance and effectiveness. Additionally, this case illustration demonstrates well how socio-cultural differences can affect the understanding of

[22] It is possible to have low socio-cultural distance between two actors from different national and cultural backgrounds who share a common organisational culture, but a high distance between two co-nationals from very different company backgrounds (Holmstrom et al., 2006, p. 2).

the game and, more importantly, the notion of (illegitimate) harm, thus shaping respective trust expectations and relationships within an organizational context.

This shows once more that GVTs, marked by socio-cultural differences among their team members, especially those that do not have a long history of working together, need some kind of behavioral orientation to align their respective (trust) expectations and actions for effective cooperation and performance. To minimize the complexity of the situation in GVTs and to create mutual reliable trust expectations, a shared understanding of (the illegitimacy) harm is thus of the utmost importance. As the ethical focal point do no (illegitimate) harm and allows people's actions to be generally more predictable and aligned, cooperation is more likely to occur. Since cooperation is the ultimate goal, it is worth investing in the ethical focal point do no (illegitimate) harm (Suchanek, 2015, p. 141).

As for GVL, it has an indispensable rile for two reasons; first, to promote trust in teams, GVL needs to create a shared understanding regarding the ethical focal point and do no (illegitimate) harm to GVTs. Second, GVL needs to act as a role model and demonstrate trustworthiness by investing itself into do no (illegitimate) harm through self-binding measures (3.2.3, 3.3). GVL should therefore self-commit to specific actions and self-retrain from others while credibly aligning communication and actions to win GVT members to equally invest into the do no harm principle for trust (Suchanek, 2015, p. 85).

The following subsection will further elaborate on that point and introduce the concept of a shared (team) mental model (SMM) as an example of common ground with regards to a shared understanding of the ethical focal point do no (illegitimate) harm for trust and thus ultimately effective cooperation and performance in GVTs.

3.2.2 The Importance of a Shared Mental Model for Trust

The previous subsection has shown that from a business ethical perspective, mutual trust expectations are formed based on a shared understanding of do no (il-) legitimate harm, which also accounts for the context of GVTs. This subsection will demonstrate how a shared understanding of the (il-)legitimacy of harm is connected to the concept of SMMs. The point of this subsection is to show that a shared understanding of the ethical focal point do no (illegitimate) harm needs an alignment of individual mental models to form an SMM.

First, the concept of (shared and team) mental models will be defined, and its function in GVTs to enhance team effectiveness clarified (Schmidtke & Cummings, 2017). Mental models (MMs) are an internal representation of knowledge that matches the situation; they consist of perceptible objects or images and abstract concepts (Johnson-Laird, 1989). Thus, MMs allow individuals to gain insight into their world by building working schemas (Maynard & Gilson, 2014, p. 8). Based on their review of organizational literature related to group cognition, Klimoski and Mohammed (1994, pp. 425–426) define team MMs as a team's shared mental construct regarding the significant components of the team's situation, including but not limited to its tasks, goals, tools, environment and working relationships like response patterns.[23] Thus, shared (team) mental models (SMMs) are a common understanding of team knowledge that members have regarding their tasks and the way they need to interact to accomplish these (Converse et al., 1993; Maynard & Gilson, 2014, p. 4). Also referred to as emergent states, SMMs reflect the cognitive, affective, and motivational states in teams (Marks et al., 2001, p. 357).[24] SMMs result from team interaction, such as team experiences and processes (Marks et al., 2001, p. 358). In this light, they represent the convergence among members' mental representations regarding various aspects of their team and task (Maynard & Gilson, 2014, p. 8).[25]

While research on SMMs has been extensively undertaken in traditional teams (Klimoski & Mohammed, 1994; Resick, Murase, et al., 2010), SMM research in VT literature has only recently begun to receive attention (Curşeu, 2006; Maynard & Gilson, 2014; Mortensen, 2014; Schmidtke & Cummings, 2017). Even though further SMMs research in GVTs needs to be done, current SMM knowledge can still be applied to GVTs due to the similarities in the processes such as sharing of information, generation of ideas, and evaluation of alternatives (Maynard & Gilson, 2014). Thus, team interactions, including VT interaction, form SMMs which, in turn, influence teamwork (Schmidtke & Cummings, 2017, pp. 660–661). This is in line with most research on SMMs in GVTs, which considers SMM development driven by increased team member interaction, communication, and training (Curşeu, 2006; Maynard & Gilson, 2014; Schmidtke & Cummings, 2017).

Regarding their function, SMMs help (global virtual) teams to better understand their environment and teamwork and enhance team performance (Converse

---

23 Research suggests that teams have multiple MMs with the two most common types being task-related and teamwork-related MMs (Klimoski & Mohammed, 1994). However, as many team functions require significant mixing between the two this MMs this differentiation has become obsolete in contemporary organisations (Schmidtke & Cummings, 2017, p. 664).

24 Marks, Mathieu, and Zaccaro (2001) term qualities or "properties of the team that are typically dynamic in nature and vary," as "emergent states" (p. 357) that reflect the cognitive, affective and motivational states in teams. (p. 358).

25 SMMs can also be coined as working schemas (Maynard & Gilson, 2014).

et al., 1993; Mathieu et al., 2000).[26] SMMs improve performance by enabling team members to make predictions built on pattern recognition, allowing for taking more appropriate actions in given situations (Maynard & Gilson, 2014, p. 8).[27] The components which affect the usefulness of MMs are complexity and accuracy (Schmidtke & Cummings, 2017, p. 663). While complexity refers to the amount of unique information represented in the MM, accuracy refers to the degree to which the MM correctly characterizes a situation (Schmidtke & Cummings, 2017, p. 665). SMMs increase in complexity due to enhanced environmental information related to the task or due to a rise in the number of team members involved as well as due to personal differences and dissimilarities in the thought processes of team members among others (Converse et al., 1993; Maynard & Gilson, 2014, p. 4). Research suggests that the more complex an SMM is with regard to a specific task, the performance on this related task decreases (Diehl & Sterman, 1995). Respectively, high SMM accuracy has been positively linked to an individual's performance on tasks related to that model (Resick, Dickson, et al., 2010). Thus, research suggests that teams with more complex and accurate shared (team) mental models demonstrate better teamwork and performance (J. Schmidtke & Cummings, 2017, p. 665).

Moreover, the accuracy of SMMs has been further specified in terms of similarity or convergence (Schmidtke & Cummings, 2017, p. 668). Similarity or convergence describes the degree to which team members share the same understanding of a given situation (Converse et al., 1993). However, suppose individual team members have divergent MMs of the same situation. In that case, the accuracy and similarity of an SMM will diminish, bearing the potential for misunderstandings, thus negatively affecting team behaviors, processes as well as team performance (Schmidtke & Cummings, 2017, p. 661).[28] Therefore, GVT research on SMMs concurs that concerning the compatibility of SMMs team members, MMs must share enough similarities "that lead to common expectations for the task and team" (Schmidtke & Cummings, 2017, p. 665).

The creation of MMs similarity in GVTs is, however, very challenging. GVTs often experience process losses compared to their face-to-face teams due to

---

[26] DeChurch and Mesmer-Magnus (2010) performed a meta-analysis of team shared cognition, including team mental models, and found a significant positive relation between the quality of teams' cognitive structures reflected in their mental models and team performance.

[27] In their research the authors found that teams involved in a flight-combat simulation that possessed convergent SMMs performed at higher levels than those that did not (Mathieu et al., 2000)

[28] Virtual collaboration may require teams to develop new types of MMs relating to communication tools for certain interactions (Schmidtke & Cummings, 2017, p. 661).

their spatial, temporal, and configurational dispersion as well as other dimensions of virtuality, which inhibit GVT members' ability to encode and share knowledge (cf. 2.2.2, cf. 2.2.3) (Schmidtke & Cummings, 2017, p. 669).[29] More specifically, different socio-cultural backgrounds further complicate the creation of an SMM in GVTs. Socio-cultural backgrounds influence the meaning and interpretation of a given situation (Agerfalk et al., 2005, p. 2), further affecting how team members react to it (Kotlarsky and Oshri, 2005) including how they interact with their teammates (Jarvenpaa & Leidner, 1999) (cf. 3.2.1). These cultural factors are all essential elements of MMs (Druskat & Pescosolido, 2002; Schmidtke & Cummings, 2017). Moreover, increasing a team's dimensions of virtuality further increases the complexities of coordinating their activities, resulting in greater difficulty in developing a shared understanding of how to accomplish tasks, thus diminishing teamwork effectiveness (Schmidtke & Cummings, 2017, p. 661). Thus, increasing levels of dimensions of virtuality are associated with an increase in the complexity of SMMs while being less accurate and convergent, thus undermining the usefulness of SMMs, which includes effective cooperation and performance in GVTs (Schmidtke & Cummings, 2017).

The fact that SMMs in GVTs are more complex and less accurate is particularly challenging for building and maintaining trust. As trust expectations are based on a shared understanding of the illegitimacy of harm (cf. 3.2.1), an SMM of the illegitimacy of harm would primarily benefit GVTs in their trust formation process. However, due to individual interpretations and socio-cultural differences which affect the understanding of the (illegitimacy) of harm, the individual MMs of the (illegitimacy) of harm may not be similar enough to be aligned. This upcoming example will present how differences in MMs regarding socio-cultural interpretations of (illegitimate) harm can negatively affect trust-building and thus team performance and effectiveness in GVTs.

The communication between GVTs members from high (e.g., United States) and low power distance cultures (e.g., Japan) differs. As a cultural dimension power structures influence the communication process (Hofstede, 1984). In low power cultures (e.g., Japan), low-status team members might be unwilling to openly disagree with high-status team members, including the leader (Hofstede, 1984). Imagine a case, where low-status members may notice that their team leader has incorrectly estimated the time to complete a particular project while distributing individual tasks that do not fit the expertise of the respective team members. low-status members from high power distance cultures will likely not

[29] See 2.1.3, definition of virtuality and dimensions of dispersion in GVTs.

voice their concerns to the leader because to do so would be culturally inappropriate and considered as being rude. They do not want to *harm* the leader, as criticizing or correcting the leader means harming them in their interpretation of harm. The overall team outcome in this example is project delay and possibly that the work is done incorrectly as tasks were not assigned to the right experts. If members are given tasks they cannot fulfill, especially in a time frame that is not adequate for the task or the team, the whole team and the leader have failed to deliver adequate results, thus undermining team effectiveness and performance. This accounts specifically for highly interdependent tasks in GVTs.

Moreover, this situation bears great potential for conflict impacting performance negatively. Members from low power distance cultures (USA) would see this kind of behavior as unreliable and unprofessional, thus misinterpreting their silence. This can create further animosities in the team with power imbalances that undermine team effectiveness and trust in the team and the leader with mutually biased assumptions. Especially with regards to the dimensions of virtuality of GVTs, including the absence of face-to-face encounters while using CMC for communication, the ground for various conflicts is great.

This example clearly shows that the ethical focal point do no (illegitimate) harm in its function to align respective trust expectations and actions needs to become a *shared understanding* between all team members, which requires an overlap of the individual MMs of (illegitimate) harm to be sufficiently compatible to act as a working SMM. Thus, in its role as an e-trust promoter (Fajen, 2018), GVL creates a shared (team) mental model based on a shared understanding of do no (illegitimate) harm for trust for effective cooperation and performance in GVTs. As trust emerges from GVT members' interactions (Curşeu, 2006, p. 249), GVL should promote and shape these interactions to enhance the trust-building process in GVTs. GVL can enhance SMM development through increased team interactions, adequate communication, and training (Curşeu, 2006; Maynard & Gilson, 2014; Resick, Murase, et al., 2010). In line with previous VT research on successful GVL and trust building GVL needs to ensure a constant flow of information while organizing regular social and professional exchange between team members and itself to further team interaction and awareness of others (Fajen, 2018, pp. 315–316, 321).

In line with that, to develop a shared working (team) mental model, GVT members should have an open discussion about content, patterns, and behavior related to that model (Schmidtke & Cummings, 2017, p. 664). Thus, regarding trust, GVL should promote an open dialogue about the illegitimacy of harm in its team while finding a consensus between all GVT members' individual and socio-culturally influenced MMs of do no (illegitimate) harm to create an SMM.[30] As information must be made explicit for the usefulness of an SMM (Schmidtke & Cummings, 2017), the consensus on the shared and agreed-on understanding of (illegitimate) harm should be openly shared and formulated into a norm. Accepted and shared communication norms build a regular pattern of interaction that supports the construction of a shared social context which promotes team cohesion in VTs (Jawadi, 2013, p. 24). Moreover, commonly formulated values and rules which are part of the corporate culture create a mutual bond in GVTs (Fajen, 2018, p. 340), thus furthering trust and effective cooperation. In this regard, GVL can incorporate the agreed-on shared understanding of the (illegitimacy) of harm into a set of guidelines visible and accessible to all GVT members. Additionally, GVL should offer specific training seminars that help create an SMM (Maynard & Gilson, 2014) that can be equally applied to the context of (the illegitimacy of) harm. Indispensable in its role in the formation of SMMs, GVL should provide training on behaviors that help the team to develop a highly accurate SMM (Resick, Dickson, et al., 2010, p. 187).

In sum, GVT members do not share the same understanding and interpretation of (the illegitimacy) of harm due to socio-cultural differences impacting how they perceive and understand given contexts. Thus, they do not have an SMM of (illegitimate) harm, which would allow them to align respective trust expectations for effective teamwork. Thus, in its role as an e-trust promoter (Fajen, 2018), GVL should create a similar and accurate enough SMM based on a shared understanding with regards to do no (illegitimate) harm for effective cooperation and performance through furthering team interaction, communication, and training with regards to that very SMM.

The following subsection will show that GVL, as an e-trust promoter, needs to role model trustworthiness through its behavior.

3.2.3 Global Virtual Leadership Needs to Role-Model Trustworthiness

The last subsection has elaborated on the importance of aligning individual MMs with regards to (the illegitimacy of) harm to create a working SMM of the latter for trust in GVTs. This subsection will show that GVL can establish the

30 Team MMs are part of group cognitive structures and are the result of individuals interacting in some social context (D'Andrade, 1981; Thompson & Fine, 1999; Wegner, 1987).

foundation for an SMM of (illegitimate) harm by establishing points and references of trustworthiness for its members by acting as a role model through its own behavior. This includes the four orientation points of commitment, integrity, consistency, and self-restraint. The point of this subsection is to underline the importance of GVL to create trust in GVTs by demonstrating trustworthiness while establishing norms, rules, and systems that foster the conditions for GVT members to invest accordingly into the ethical focal point do no (illegitimate) harm for trust.

As Fajen's (2018) empirical study demonstrates, the novel, challenging leadership situation of GVTs, characterized by a high degree of complexity, results in multiple roles and complex tasks for the leader, especially concerning diffusing conflicts. This shows that adequate and explicit leadership is indispensable in GVTs (Fajen, 2018, p. 331). In general, leadership needs to make quick and pragmatic decisions under contingent complex conditions that often contradict ethical reflections (Suchanek, 2015, p. 279). These contingent conditions are even more complex in GVTs than in traditional teams (cf. 2.3.2.) and give rise to many challenges that bear great potential for conflicts (cf. 2.3.2., 2.3.3.).

Conflicts undermining trust and effective cooperation arise rapidly and regularly in all kinds of GVTs (Köppel, 2007; Mortensen & Hinds, 2001; O'Leary & Mortensen, 2010). The cause of virtual conflicts relates to weak interpersonal bonds between dispersed members, the lack of a shared context and mutual knowledge, and failure of information exchange leading to various misunderstandings and miscommunication in the team (Cramton, 2001; Hinds & Bailey, 2003). Some researchers even argue that GVTs encounter higher levels of conflict, especially interpersonal and task-based conflict (Cramton, 2001; Herbsleb et al., 2000; Köppel, 2007).[31] Regarding interpersonal conflicts, the failures of information exchange often lead to personal attribution and judgments about other team members rather than situational attributions (Cramton, 2001, p. 365). Further accentuated by socio-cultural differences, intercultural and intra-team conflicts often occur in GVTs emerging from us-versus-them attitudes based on ethnocentrism and stereotypes between GVT members located at different sites (Köppel, 2007, pp. 286–291). These conflicts often lead to less effective and performing GVTs due to limited information flow, project delays, reduced team cohesion, and faulty attributions (Cramton, 2001; Hinds & Bailey, 2003). According to VT literature, this magnified potential for conflicts requires GVL to anticipate and

[31] This relates to the fact that conflicts in GVTs often remain unidentified and unaddressed for long periods of time (Morrison-Smith & Ruiz, 2020).

mitigate conflicts before they impact team effectiveness negatively while accommodating each team member's socio-emotional needs and establishing consensus (Fajen, 2018, p. 281).

Moreover, as a leader, one of the most important tasks is persuading others to cooperate effectively (Suchanek, 2010, p. 280). As such, leaders must avoid or defuse relevant conflict areas (Fajen, 2018). GVT research suggests that due to the magnified potential of conflict in GVTs, GVL must have a good understanding of its team members to mitigate these conflicts (cf. 2.3.3). From a leadership ethical perspective, conflicts arise due to the tension between morality and self-interest (Carson, 2003). To further understand this tension within an organizational context, Suchanek gives insights and definitions (2010, pp. 279–283). Morality is a kind of individual betterment that simultaneously serves the goal of long-term corporate value enhancement and social value creation (Suchanek, 2013, p. 338). Thus, morality refers to normative principles and values, such as do no harm and trust. The concept of self-interest integrates the totality of empirical (incentive) conditions (Suchanek, 2013, p. 335).

From a leadership ethical point of view, leaders need to acknowledge human beings as moral subjects who have dignity and are endowed with freedom while being subject to empirical—biological, psychological, and social conditions, among others (Miller, 2003). This inherent human condition gives rise to a multitude of varying self-interests that can sharply contrast a team's established norms and values, thus harboring the potential for various conflicts. Therefore, to resolve these conflicts, morality and self-interest need to be reconciled (Suchanek, 2013)[32]. Leaders should be aware that humans can orient their actions towards general normative principles and values and, at the same time, towards situational incentives, which can give rise to short-term opportunistic behavior undermining trust and thus effective cooperation (Suchanek, 2013, p. 335).

In line with that, prior VT research advises GVL to engage intensively with all individual team members (Jarvenpaa & Leidner, 1999). Even though this is a demanding and time-consuming task successful virtual leadership should frequently be in touch with its GVT members to be able to respond to their personalities and employ them according to their abilities while taking sociocultural differences into account, which impact communication, among others (Fajen, 2018, pp. 280–281).[33] It should be noted that due to limited individual

---

[32] These conflicts between morality and self-interest can also be referred to as "inconsistencies" which will find further explanation in the following paragraphs (Suchanek, 2013).

[33] GVL needs to develop a sense for the personalities present in the team, for example for introverts and extroverts, and their respective skills.

resources and time constraints as presented above, many global virtual leaders fail to comply with this task, as they simply do not have the energy and the time to fulfill all the task- and employee-orientated roles. This is well summarized by the following statement of a global virtual leader:

> "Well, first of all [the challenge is] time. It's still time even though it's virtual and [...] I can achieve 50 % more than I would have 20 years ago; still, time is a huge issue. I feel I could use 3 or 4 more hours every day." (Fajen, 2018, p. 283)

Moreover, the ethical focal point do no (illegitimate) harm as an essential normative point of orientation and action can support leadership in dealing with conflicts (Entschew & Suchankek, 2019). It can first serve for leaders as a guideline for their own actions. Furthermore, leaders need to motivate employees (and coordinate their actions accordingly) to invest in the sense of the ethical focal point do no (illegitimate) harm for their own well-understood benefit, that of the company and ultimately also of society (Suchanek, 2013, p. 336).[34] Thus, to decrease the potential for conflicts, GVL should introduce a token of trustworthiness and reliability for effective cooperation through their own behavior and lead by example to motivate others to follow. In this regard, leaders need to organize the conditions of trustworthiness concerning their own behavior and concerning norms, rules, and systems (Suchanek, 2013, pp. 337–338).

With regards to a leader's own behavior, the following four points of orientation represent signs of trustworthy behavior of the leader and provide the basis for the willingness of team members to make specific investments in line with the ethical focal point do no (illegitimate) harm: *(self-) commitment, integrity, avoiding relevant inconsistencies,* and *self-restraint* (Suchanek, 2013, p. 339). After shortly introducing these concepts, a real-life example of a GVT context will be given to underpin further the importance and practicability of these concepts for GVL, GVTs, and trust.

Firstly, the concept of *commitment* and the interrelated concept of *integrity* are introduced. Commitment is a promise or firm decision to do something and implies a willingness to give time and energy to something or somebody (Cambridge Dictionary, 2014). Suchanek (2013) further specifies commitment as the ability of leadership to credibly realize normative foundations of its own leadership behavior or corporate constitution, as expressed in the fundamental orientation points of the company with regards to vision, mission statement, and

---

[34] However, given the countless challenges of everyday business life like budget restrictions, time, competitive pressures, multiple conflicts of interest, uncertainties, complex and fragmented value-added structures this is a highly demanding task (Suchanek, 2015).

principles and values (p. 339). Commitment is clarified and manifested in one's communication and actions (Suchanek, 2013, p. 339).

Moreover, *integrity* is the basis of reliability and, consequently, trustworthiness (Suchanek, 2013, p. 339). Integrity refers to "the extent to which a trustee is believed to adhere to sound moral and ethical principles, with synonyms including fairness, justice, consistency, and promise fulfillment" (Colquitt et al., 2007, p. 910). Introduced as one of the most significant core characteristics of successful leaders in both business and leadership ethics literature (Badaracco & Ellsworth, 1989), integrity has been proven to highly influence the trust-building process in teams (Colquitt et al., 2007, p. 918). Built up and maintained as an intangible asset' integrity requires investments (Suchanek, 2013, p. 339). The fundamental characteristic of integrity lies in the overarching consistency and coherence of values and everyday practice, communication, and actions (Suchanek & von Broock, 2008).

Furthermore, the following orientation refers to *avoiding relevant inconsistencies*. This refers to situations in which fundamental normative orientation points (values, principles) are in apparent contradiction, or more precisely, are perceived as such, with the actual decisions or actions of leadership or team members (Suchanek, 2013, p. 340).[35] These areas of conflict between morals and self-interest are mentioned earlier in this subsection, undermining trust and thus effective cooperation.

Finally, the fourth point of orientation for trustworthy behavior is (individual or collective) *self-restraint* which can help leaders to deal with these relevant inconsistencies (Suchanek, 2013, p. 340). Self-restraint refers to structures, rules, or dispositions that make certain options for action impossible or sufficiently unattractive for an (individual or corporate) actor in a concrete situation. These options would lead to conflicts between morality and self-interest (Suchanek, 2013, p. 340). The basis of this concept is the fact that in certain situations, it would be an excessive demand on the individual—the employee or the leader-to resolve concrete conflicts of morals and self-interest in favor of morals if this would entail severe disadvantages (Suchanek, 2013, p. 340).[36]

The common denominator between the concepts of (self-) commitment, integrity, avoiding relevant inconsistencies, and self-restraint as signals of trustworthiness is an *alignment* between *communication and consequent actions.*

---

[35] Differences between communication and action can also cause relevant inconsistencies.

[36] Certain demands do not stand the test of everyday due to a lack of incentive compatibility as no one will at least not systematically and permanently act against their own self-interest (Suchanek, 2013, p. 341).

However, due to the given empirical conditions of everyday business life, situations often occur in which such conflicts between communication and actions are practically unavoidable (Suchanek, 2013, pp. 340–341).[37] A significant reason for this is that the communication of values and other normative orientation points are linked to expectations that cannot be fulfilled under the given conditions (Suchanek, 2013).[38] These conditions are further accentuated in the context of GVTs due to differences in understanding of the (illegitimacy) of harm (cf. 3.2.1) and a non-alignment of individual mental models concerning the latter (cf. 3.2.2), hampering the creation of trust and effective cooperation.[39]

One of the most cited examples of relevant inconsistencies within an organizational context concerns the lacking role model function of leadership, while another one relates to the lack of coordination (Suchanek, 2013, p. 342). The following example intertwines both of these relevant inconsistencies and shows how trust and effective cooperation in GVTs can be undermined if the communication and actions of GVL differ. As already elaborated in previous examples, one of the tasks of GVL is to find joint meeting windows for all GVT members. GVL is required to set up meetings that suit all members. GVL can, therefore, not make people regularly participate very early or very late and must find a compromise between all time schedules of its members (Fajen, 2018, p. 272). Imagine the case in which GVL does not comply with this rule and organizes the meetings with regard to the convenience of their own timetable.

Moreover, even though the company's mission statement states inclusion and respect as its main values, GVL does not stick to these values in its actions by organizing a meeting where important decisions are made without some of the GVT members being present due to an incompatibility of joint time frames. This case of intertwined relevant inconsistencies has been shown in prior VT research to happen regularly due to the geographical and structural dispersion of GVT members (O'Leary & Mortensen, 2010). Thus, members at isolated or imbalanced sites are often excluded from decisions leaving them left alone, thus undermining trust and effective cooperation in GVTs (O'Leary & Mortensen, 2010).

---

[37] These include budget restrictions, time and competitive pressures, misunderstandings and lack of information, conflicts of interest amongst others.

[38] Various stakeholders of a company have heterogeneous and partly incompatible interests and expectations, some of which are also considered justified and thus non-negotiable by the respective stakeholder (Suchanek, 2013, p. 341).

[39] Trust expectations arise from individual understandings and interpretations of harm which are related to socio-cultural concepts (cf. 3.2.1).

As there are many more possible inconsistencies that can occur in GVTs, it is the central task of leadership to specify and reduce these areas of conflict to allow GVT members to invest in the ethical focal point do no (illegitimate) harm for trust to enhance performance.[40] GVL can reduce the likelihood of conflicts by managing trust perceptions and by fostering adequate framework conditions for GVT members to invest accordingly into the ethical focal point do no (illegitimate) harm. According to Mayer et al.'s (1995) integrative model of trustworthiness, trust is built and evaluated on members' perceptions of ability, benevolence, and integrity. This also accounts for a global virtual context (Flavian et al., 2019; Ford et al., 2017). Thus, virtual leadership should strategically manage these perceptions to build trust levels through what they do and how they do it (Ford et al., 2017, p. 3).

With regards to adequate framework conditions for trust leaders are required to set conditions including appropriate rules (compliance), incentive systems, and control and sanction mechanisms, amongst others (Suchanek, 2013, p. 341) (3.3.3).[41] GVT literature encourages GVL to establish rules concerning task accomplishment, modus operandi, and communication to underpin the creation of trust relationships in GVTs (Jarvenpaa & Leidner, 1999, pp. 807–813). Moreover, GVL should establish communication rules concerning the time frame in which GVT members are required to answer to reduce prevailing ambiguities (Ford et al., 2017, p. 4). With regards to the example mentioned above on finding a joint meeting window in GVTs, Fajen's empirical research concluded that successful GVL sets up at least two meetings at different times suitable for most GVT members (Fajen, 2018, p. 272). In line with other VT research effective GVL should go the extra mile and put in more work and time than traditional leaders to accommodate the needs of all GVT members and stakeholders involved (Hoch & Kozlowski, 2014; Jawadi, 2013; Kayworth & Leidner, 2002). Furthermore, communication rules and patterns have especially been promoted as of the utmost importance in creating trust in GVTs (Marlow et al., 2017, p. 7) (cf. 3.2.2).

Thus, to build trust, leaders must have design capacities to create the framework conditions alongside argumentation competencies (Suchanek, 2013). In line with previous GVT research, GVL needs to have not only outstanding communication capacities but also intercultural competencies, which include the capacity

[40] Not all inconsistencies can be resolved. Many conditions that lead to these inconsistencies cannot be shaped or can only be shaped to a limited extent due to costs or other contingencies (Suchanek, 2013, 2015).

[41] Subsection 3.3.3 offers more examples with regards to framework conditions for trust.

to transmit the same information in different ways to different people to get the same message across (Fajen, 2018, pp. 321–324) (cf. 2.3.2). GVT research concludes that virtual leaders' communication capacities are the most essential skills for successful GVL (Fajen, 2018, p. 347; Kayworth & Leidner, 2000, p. 189). Thus, in its role as an e-communicator, GVL has to mitigate conflicts and accommodate the interests of all parties while building consensus (Fajen, 2018, p. 281). GVL has to find a compromise which it can do by promoting a continuous virtual dialogue that underlines GVL's role as e-decision, e-responsibility maker as well as e-communicator (Fajen, 2018, pp. 320–321).

Moreover, leaders and their behavior are the most important representations of their goals (Badaracco & Ellsworth, 1989). Thus, it is of the utmost importance that GVL aligns their words and actions for trust in GVTs. Especially with regards to the above elaborated four orientation points of trustworthiness, namely (self-) commitment, integrity, avoidance of relevant inconsistencies, and self-restraint, leaders are advised to lead by example (Suchanek, 2013). These points can be equally applied to a global virtual leadership context and are aligned with prior GVT research regarding trust. Norman et al.'s (2019) research on trust in GVTs has shown that the most common leadership traits and competencies for trust are communication competencies, integrity, honesty, openness, relationships both inside and outside of work, time and the leader's competence, knowledge, abilities, intelligence and experience and especially "congruence between espoused and enacted values" (Norman et al., 2019, p. 290). This is in line with leadership ethics literature that emphasizes the importance of consistency and coherence of values and everyday practice, communication, and actions (Suchanek & von Broock, 2008).

The leader-follower relationship is crucial for trust-building in a virtual context, including the leader's and the follower's personal characteristics, depth of relationship, and time (Norman et al., 2019). Moreover, Fajen's empirical study has shown that GVL and GVT members alike both confirm the importance of GVL acting as a role model as of the utmost importance for successful GVTs (Fajen, 2018, p. 355). Based on Flavian's research, GVL's behavioral (and even physical) characteristics exert a positive and significant effect on trust in GVL, which in turn influences organizational efficiency (Flavian et al., 2019, p. 12).

This confirms that individual self-commitment to leadership is one of the most elementary foundations of successful and responsible leadership (Suchanek, 2013, p. 341) and can equally be applied to a virtual organizational context. The purpose of self-commitment is the establishment of reliable signals whose credibility also depends on their sufficient clarity and comprehensibility (Suchanek, 2013, pp. 340–341).[42] Alignment between communication and consequent actions is thus a matter of credibility. Leaders do not only need to realize these trustworthy behaviors, but they need to be perceived as credible in doing so by their members (Flavian et al., 2019). Flavian (2019) confirms the importance of GVT members' perception of their leader as being empathetic and exerting justice, influencing the trust-building process in GVTs (Flavian et al., 2019, p. 3).

Finally, leaders are advised to convince GVT members to self-commit and invest in the ethical focal point do no (illegitimate) harm; for their own well-understood self-interest, that of the company, and according to their own moral concepts (Suchanek, 2015). This point is aligned with GVL's role as an e-motivator, showcasing good argumentative and reasoning ability to inspire GVT members to follow the leader's lead by showing them respect and appreciation (Fajen, 2018, p. 317)[43]. As for the trust process in GVTs, it is of the utmost importance that leaders generate enthusiasm for achieving common goals and motivate members to invest in these, especially at the beginning of a project (Jarvenpaa & Leidner, 1999, pp. 807–813). This is in line with prior research on transformational leadership behavior for virtual leadership success, which includes leadership commitment increases workers' self-perceived employability, performance, and self-commitment to the organization in general (Purvanova & Bono, 2009; Yahaya & Ebrahim, 2016).

In sum, this subsection has demonstrated that to build trust, GVL has to diffuse conflicts in GVTs while establishing norms, rules, and systems that foster the conditions for GVT members to invest accordingly into the ethical focal point do no (illegitimate) harm for trust. To further inspire GVT members, GVL should act as a role model and demonstrate trustworthiness by adhering to the four points of orientation of trustworthy behavior, namely (self-) commitment, integrity, avoidance of relevant inconsistencies, and self-restraint while adhering itself to the set framework conditions that foster trust.

The next chapter will introduce the third order of the heuristical tool of practical syllogism with regards to (3) investment. This point will merge the previous

[42] It is important to note that self-commitment comes with costs. On the one hand, there are opportunity costs in the sense that self-restraint also excludes individual options for action that would have brought advantages for oneself without having disadvantages for others (Suchanek, 2013, pp. 340–341). On the other hand, the organisation of self-restraint entails costs e.g. the establishment of a compliance system to check compliance with standards, the establishment and, if necessary, implementation of sanction mechanisms, the corresponding training of employees and others (Suchanek, 2013, pp. 340–341).

[43] To do this, they must create an incentive system adapted to the global virtual context, consisting of monetary and non-monetary incentives (Fajen, 2018).

chapters regarding GVL and trust-building and answer the research question of how GVL can actively promote trust in GVTs. It will be shown that GVL can do so by investing itself into trust by realizing do no (illegitimate) harm. Regarding that, the heuristical business ethical model of good leadership by Suchanek (2019) will be introduced.

3.3 Investment: Self-Binding Measures for Future Benefits

This last subchapter represents the third order of the practical syllogism and elaborates on the (3) investment concept. This third step integrates both (1) normative and (2) empirical levels and (3) answers the question *"What should I/we do?"* (Suchanek, 2015c, p. 48). The first order with regards to (1) values answers the question *"What do I/we want?"* which in the case of this thesis refers to leading GVT successfully by enabling effective cooperation (cf. 3.1.1) following the golden rules' do no harm dimension (cf. 3.1.2), and more precisely, the ethical focal point do no (illegitimate) harm for trust (cf. 3.1.3). The second order refers to the reality of trust-building in GVTs and answers the question "*What can I/we do?*" summarizing the challenges of trust-building with regards to differences in understanding of trust and respective trust expectations due to the lack of a shared understanding of the illegitimacy of harm as part of the overall communication challenge in GVTs. Thus, GVL, in its role as an e-trust promoter, should create an SMM of the (illegitimacy) of harm (cf. 3.2.2) based on a shared understanding between all GVT members to align trust expectations and actions (cf. 3.2.1) while further role-modeling trustworthiness through its own behavior including setting the right framework conditions (cf. 3.2.3).

Role modeling trustworthy behaviors are (3) examples of investments that realize (1) values and principles while (2) confronting the given conditions of reality. Thus, legitimate expectations and corresponding investments that bring the best possible outcome regarding the first order (1) can be derived. Therefore, the practical syllogism allows to "convey realism to ethics, but also, conversely, to not forget values in the world of facts and practical constraints" (Suchanek, 2015, p. 46; own translation). This chapter represents the quintessence of this dissertation and answers the research question: *how can GVL actively promote trust and create common ground regarding mutual reliable trust expectations in socio-culturally diverse GVTs?* [44] The point of this thesis is that GVL, in its role as an e-trust promoter (Fajen, 2018, p. 318), [45] can realize trust in GVTs by investing itself into trust by applying the ethical focal point do no (illegitimate) harm. This argument will be elucidated after defining the concept of investment by further elaborating on the investments that GVL should realize for trust. These are structured and based on the business ethical model of good leadership (Suchanek, 2019), which will be further underpinned by previous VT key findings (Fajen, 2018; Ford et al., 2017; Jarvenpaa & Leidner, 1999; Maynard & Gilson, 2014; Schmidtke & Cummings, 2017).

First, with regards to *investment*, from a business ethical perspective, this concept can be broadly defined as such: "[A]n investment involves the use of one's freedom and depends on one's intentions and capabilities. Often, investing is tantamount to doing something one is not keen on doing now but expects to appreciate later, thereby avoiding future regretfulness" (Suchanek, 2017, p. 83). The concept of investment refers to doing or not doing something and relates to one's own behavior (Suchanek, 2015, p. 48). Investments include consequences of actions and conditions for (future) actions and respective consequences for and of future actions (Suchanek, 2015, p. 49). These investments include the organization, maintenance, or acceptance of conducive conditions and avoiding detrimental conditions (Suchanek, 2015).

Trust has been elucidated as the most crucial factor for social cooperation (cf. 3.1.1), and the *ethical focal point do no (illegitimate) harm* as the most fundamental *trust expectation* (cf. 3.1.3, cf. 3.2.1). Consequently, investments that raise awareness for and prevent illegitimate harm can improve (future) conditions for a trustful cooperation. Investments that serve the purpose of promoting trustful cooperation for mutual advantage require actions to be coordinated (Suchanek, 2015). As an essential prerequisite for successful cooperation for mutual advantage, points of orientation or focal points as simple, robust, and (therefore) generally accepted means of coordination of actions should be established (Suchanek, 2015, pp. 140–141). Especially with regards to GVTs and their dynamic and complex structure, these focal points provide references or signals

---

[44] This chapter will answer this question by merging the previous subchapters with regards to the specific roles and competencies of leadership for trust, trust as the condition for successful leadership in GVTs (cf. 2.3.3) as elaborated previously by VT literature, as well as business ethical reflections as laid out and explicitly elucidated in the context of GVTs with regards to the first order (3.1) and the second-order (3.2).

[45] The definition of an e-trust promoter based on Fajen's (2018) research is given in cf. 2.3.2.

that can support leadership and teams in trust-building and thus further effective cooperation and enhance performance (cf. 3.1.3).

The two main forms of focal points are, on the one hand, normative points such as ethical focal points, e.g., do no illegitimate harm, to define shared goals, values, and interests, and on the other hand, empirical focal points, such as rules which are important for the concretization and coordination of actions (Suchanek, 2015, pp. 142–143). These focal points can align respective trust expectations of trustor and trustee and function as a guideline for one's own behavior bringing about successful cooperation; thus, it is worth investing in them (Suchanek, 2015, pp. 141–143). Trust relationships' three essential focal points are promises, rules, and values (Suchanek, 2015, p. 143). With regards to GVT literature, the importance of investing in trust through creating points of orientation that guide behavior and expectations in GVTs has been well summarized in Ford's (2017) conclusion: "While the technology is the hardware of creating virtual trust, the actions (or lack of actions) of the parties in virtual teams are the software that builds and sustains the needed trust" (p. 3). Thus, the organization, the leader, and individual team members must invent ways to be transparent with each other to build and sustain trust (Ford et al., 2017, p. 3).

These focal points are embedded in the business ethical model of good leadership (Suchanek, 2019), which offers a hands-on guideline for leaders to realize trust in (global virtual) teams. According to this model (global virtual), leaders should invest themselves in trust by investing into do no (illegitimate) harm resulting in individual actions and expectations for leadership alongside the following four dimensions:

1) showing *respect* to GVT members (3.3.1),
2) providing a frame of *orientation* for GVT members by creating a shared (team) mental model of illegitimate harm (3.3.2),
3) *setting conditions* for trust (3.3.3),
4) acting as a *role model* through trustworthy behavior while showing consistency in communication and actions (3.3.4)

This thesis contributes with new findings for GVL, trust, and effective cooperation in GVT by merging business ethical concepts and prior GVT literature highlighting GVL's indispensable role in the trust-building process in GVTs, further enriching the definition of GVL's unique role as an active e-trust promoter by offering a practical guideline to realize trust in GVTs.[46]

3.3.1 Respect

First, good leadership invests in trust by showing respect to team members.
The value of respect is the basis and a function of trust (Suurendonk, 2022). Even though the concept of Respect is a difficult one to grasp, attempts to do so have given rise to a multitude of interpretations, with one of the most prominent one emanating from German moral philosopher Immanuel Kant (1785), summarized in his second formulation of the categorical imperative as: "So act that you treat humanity, whether in your own person or the person of any other, always at the same time as an end, never merely as a means" (p. 429).[47] Accordingly, one of the most basic means of making reciprocal contributions to a (more) successful life is showing mutual Respect and appreciation (Suchanek, 2015, p. 156). Respecting another person means thus taking their legitimate trust expectations into account (Suchanek, 2015, p. 157), which means not to be (illegitimately) harmed. This mutual respect is essential "because our own expectation of not being harmed by others requires us to afford others the same treatment" (WCGE, 2017, p. 5).

Respect is a fundamental ethical value that manifests as an attitude based on frames and abilities that can be learned and practiced. Thus, respect can be invested in (Suchanek, 2019). Regarding the function of values and, more specifically, the value of Respect as a focal point, it can bring about superior forms of cooperation due to reduced transaction costs (Suchanek, 2015, p. 154). This is because shared values are the core of a shared understanding of the game allowing coordinating cooperative ventures (Suchanek, 2015, p. 154). Furthermore, respecting others makes cooperative ventures easier if they are convinced that their interests and opinions will be respected and that their person, views, and opinions are valued (Suchanek, 2015, p. 156).

Concrete examples of demonstrating respect are active listening, putting oneself in the shoes of the other, giving constructive feedback, keeping promises,

---

[46] These four points of orientation have already been individually elaborated on in the previous chapters and further underpinned by VT literature findings and are summarized in this chapter.

[47] It is important to distinguish between respect for a person's performance and respect for the person her/himself. The latter is the form of respect which is needed for trustful cooperation in the sense of this dissertation.

adhering to laws amongst others—and, first and foremost, avoiding doing (illegitimate) harm in words and actions (Suchanek, 2019). This general attitude of respect toward GVT members has been highlighted numerous times by GVT research as a prerequisite for successful GVL (Fajen, 2018; Ford et al., 2017; Jarvenpaa et al., 2004; Jarvenpaa & Leidner, 1999; Purvanova & Bono, 2009). Successful GVT leaders show respect and, as such, demonstrate an appreciation of each individual, proactively reach out to their team members and strive for regular exchanges despite long distances (Fajen, 2018, p. 334). GVL is encouraged to create personal relationships with all members, especially at the beginning of the cooperation (Jarvenpaa & Leidner, 1999), and to "socialize" (Jarvenpaa et al., 2004, p. 263). GVL can do so through regular one-to-ones and visits of team members at their location (Fajen, 2018, pp. 333–334). By creating individual personal relationships based on fairness and politeness, GVL can also motivate team members individually based on precise expectation management, as well as transparent allocation of resources and tasks (Fajen, 2018, pp. 352–354).

Moreover, GVL is encouraged to send cues of its trustworthiness to team members by recognizing the unique challenges they encounter (Ford et al., 2017, p. 7). Thus, GVL should spend the time and energy to accommodate each member's individual circumstances and be sensitive to their personal needs (Ford et al., 2017, pp. 7–8). It is advised that global virtual leaders exercise elements of a transformational leadership style to ensure effective cooperation in GVTs and, as such, are recommended to treat each team member as an individual taking into account their different personalities, their socio-cultural backgrounds as well as the specific framework conditions of their work (Fajen, 2018, pp. 333–334; Purvanova & Bono, 2009).[48] This is particularly important concerning giving constructive and regular feedback which is positively linked to trust in GVTs (Jarvenpaa & Leidner, 1999).

Furthermore, GVL can respect these differences in GVTs by offering tailor-made programs such as language lessons to those not speaking the predominant working language or showing interest and appreciation of national celebrations or holidays at virtual team member locations or offering rotating times for team meetings to accommodate different time zones (Ford et al., 2017, pp. 5–7).

Thus, in its role as an active e-trust promoter, good and successful GVL shows Respect in words and action to all GVT members.

[48] Based on Bass and Avolio's (1993) theory on transformational leadership. It should be noted that GVL is equally encouraged to exercise a transactional leadership style, depending on the situation and circumstance.

3.3.2 Orientation

Second, good leadership invests in trust by providing focal points for orientation.[49] The ethical focal point do no (illegitimate) harm has been introduced as the main condition for trust as it forms respective trust expectations between a trustor and trustee, thus serving as point of orientation (cf. 3.2.1).[50] As common ground between GVT members do no (illegitimate) harm can align and coordinate respective trust expectations and actions if it is a shared understanding thus supporting leaders in dealing with conflict situations (Suchanek & Entschew, 2018, p. 224)(cf. 3.1.3). The creation of this shared understanding with regards to do no (illegitimate) harm needs an alignment of individual MMs and an overlap of certain critical information among all team members to be sufficiently compatible with acting as a working SMM (cf. 3.2.2) An SMM helps (global virtual) teams to better understand their environment and teamwork and enhances team performance (Schmidtke & Cummings, 2017, p. 664). In this regard, GVL should strategically employ team member interaction, communication, and training, which supports the creation of SMM in GVTs (Maynard & Gilson, 2014, p. 4).

In line with that, GVL needs to promote regular exchange between team members in its role of e-knot, e-communicator, and e-networker to further team interaction and awareness of others' tasks and accomplishments which is essential for trust in GVTs (Fajen, 2018, pp. 315–316, 321). Thus, while furthering an open discussion about what its members' shared understanding of their interactions will be, GVL has the task of finding a consensus between all GVT members' individual and socio-culturally influenced MMs of do no (illegitimate) harm (cf. 3.2.2) and make sure that team members share enough similarity that leads to common expectations for the task and team (Schmidtke & Cummings, 2017, p. 665).

Moreover, as for the usefulness of an SMM in GVTs, the agreed information and understanding of the content (Schmidtke & Cummings, 2017), which in the case of this thesis refers to the illegitimacy of harm for trust, has to be made explicit (cf. 3.2.2). Commonly formulated values and norms foster the creation of a mutual bond in GVTs thus furthering trust and effective cooperation (Fajen, 2018, p. 340). GVL can incorporate the shared understanding of the illegitimacy

---

[49] Schelling defined focal points as elements "of each person's expectation of what the other expects him to expect to be expected to do" (Schelling, 1980, p. 57).

[50] The trust relationship between two interacting parties is based on the trust game (Kreps, 1990).

of harm as a value and rule into the corporate culture to create a useful SMM for trust (cf. 3.2.2).

Regarding rules, they are essential as they structure everyday life and support the development of expectations about others' future conditions of action while being a focal point for one's own behavior (Suchanek, 2015, p. 144). In this sense, rules engender mutual behavioral reliability and allow social cooperation, especially with regard to conflict situations (Suchanek, 2015, p. 148).[51] For this reason, it is simply necessary to invest in rules (Suchanek, 2015, p. 152).

Accepted and shared communication norms build regular patterns of interaction in GVTs which support the construction of a shared social context furthering team cohesion (Jawadi, 2013, p. 24). Thus, an SMM of the illegitimacy of harm formulated into a norm can support GVT members in building reliable behavioral patterns, therefore, furthering trust and effective cooperation (cf. 3.2.2). Additionally, specific training seminars enhance the effectiveness of an SMM (Maynard & Gilson, 2014), GVL should offer special education and coaching with regards to the illegitimacy of harm in their teams.

Finally, GVL should demonstrate the ethical focal point do no (illegitimate) harm by acting as a role model in communication and action (cf. 3.2.3). By doing so, GVL can more easily convince GVT members to equally self-commit to the ethical focal point do no (illegitimate) harm (Suchanek, 2010, p. 286). This point will be further elaborated on in 3.3.4.

Thus, in its role as an active e-trust promoter, good and successful GVL provides orientation for GVTs for effective cooperation by creating a shared (team) mental model based on a shared understanding of do no (illegitimate) harm being integrated into rule.

3.3.3 Set Conditions

Third, good leadership invests in trust by setting up the right framework conditions. These conditions include, among others, appropriate rules (compliance), incentive systems, control, and sanction mechanisms, setting, clarifying, and fairly applying standards for performance, and formulating appropriate expectations (Suchanek, 2019). Furthermore, they include recruiting, promoting, and developing staff, organizing information exchange, communication and reflection, providing support in conflict situations, and especially by avoiding (relevant) inconsistencies

[51] Rules however depend on their proper understanding. They need to be understood and accepted by those who comply to them to develop an effect (Suchanek, 2015, p. 152).

(between rules, promises, and values on the one hand and own decisions, performance targets or concrete expectations of action on the other (Suchanek, 2019). These points find further resonance within GVT literature and have been stressed as of the utmost importance for effective collaboration in GVTs (Fajen, 2018; Ford et al., 2017; Jarvenpaa & Leidner, 1999; Jawadi, 2013; Treinen & Miller-Frost, 2006).

Moreover, with regards to standards of performance and expectations, GVT literature suggests that key elements leading to high trust in GVTs include leaders setting clear goals and distributing tasks, as well as offering fast and constructive feedback (Fajen, 2018, p. 104; Jarvenpaa & Leidner, 1999; Jawadi, 2013, p. 20) (cf. 2.3.3). This refers to global virtual leaders roles of an e-organizer and an e-coordinator (Fajen, 2018, p. 317). As such, they have to realize complex organizational and coordination tasks, including creating common and individual goals, providing transnational visions, developing strategies, and setting priorities, amongst others (Fajen, 2018, p. 317).

Moreover, GVL is encouraged to set direct individual performance measures to reward or discipline those who comply or do not comply with the set standard, which is key for trust (Ford et al., 2017, p. 8) to keep the integrity of the group (Jarvenpaa et al., 1998). Team members that do not comply with the rules should not have any benefits in comparison to those that do abide by the rules. Thus, investing in non-monetary incentives such as training opportunities and praise and recognition by GVL are particularly recommended to reward team members (Gobeli et al., 2012, p. 262). This refers to GVL's exercise of the role of an e-controller which includes checking and evaluating individual and team performance to give the team members orientation (Fajen, 2018, p. 320).

Furthermore, regarding recruiting, promoting, and developing staff (cf. 2.3.3), GVL is advised to properly select and prepare GVT members as team composition plays a crucial role in trust-building (Ford et al., 2017, pp. 4–5). Team member's willingness to trust and a positive view of the organization (Ford et al., 2017, p. 9) as well as their personality and values, including their ability, integrity, competence, fairness, honesty, openness, and level of autonomy in their respective teams influence trust in GVTs (Choi & Cho, 2019) (cf. 2.3.3.). Moreover, in their role as an e-developer global virtual leader are advised to set conditions that ensure the continuous development of each individual team member and offer various learning and development programs (Fajen, 2018, p. 319). Prior VT research has shown the positive effect of these development programs on different levels of teamwork (Jawadi, 2013; Treinen & Miller-Frost, 2006). GVL should, for example, invest in basic cultural awareness training for its team at the beginning of projects to mitigate any possible communication problems

(Treinen & Miller-Frost, 2006). GVT research has shown that members who received communication training were found to achieve better task-related team results, practiced more open and honest interactions, showed a higher commitment to achieving given goals and more importantly showed a higher level of trust (Fajen, 2018).

Moreover, leaders can invest in trust by organizing information exchange, communication, and reflection (Suchanek, 2019). This point is especially important within a global virtual organizational context. Leaders have to compensate for the lack of formal and informal communication in GVTs by actively promoting regular professional and social information exchange between team members and themselves for the building of trust (Jarvenpaa & Leidner, 1999) (cf. 2.3.3).[52] Trust has been positively linked to team awareness and as such GVL is advised to foster collective awareness through both activity and social awareness which reduces GVT members' insecurity and ambiguities and contributes to the building of team cohesion which is of the utmost importance for trust (Daassi et al., 2010) (cf. 2.3.3). This is in line with GVL's role as an e-knot, an e-networker and an e-communicator who promotes a constant flow of information necessary for GVT members to stay aware while organizing regular social interaction to ultimately foster effective cooperation (Fajen, 2018, pp. 315–321).

Also, good, and successful leadership handles conflict situations in GVTs (cf. 3.2.3). GVL is required to resolve professional and personal disagreements (Ford et al., 2017, p. 7). In their role as an employee-oriented e-supporter, GVL should proactively diffuse conflicts, especially those that arise due to cultural differences, and mediate between the respective parties (Fajen, 2018, p. 319). Moreover, by supporting its members' socio-emotional needs which is key to build trust in GVTs, GVL can mitigate conflicts early by reading in between the lines and anticipating potential problems (Ford et al., 2017, p. 5) (cf. 3.2.3). GVL can do so by engaging intensively with all team members to respond to their needs and personalities (Fajen, 2018, p. 334). It should be noted that GVL does not have unlimited capacities and resources to take care of all members with that much care, even if they should and wish to do so. One should not put too much pressure on GVL or too many expectations and thus equally respect GVL's personal, emotional and physical boundaries.

Thus, in its role as an active e-trust promoter good and successful GVL sets up appropriate framework conditions in line with the ethical focal point do no

[52] Communication in co-located teams often takes place unconsciously, whereas digital communication must be consciously initiated using the most suitable communication medium for the current occasion (Fajen, 2018, p. 324)(cf. 2.3.3.).

(illegitimate) harm with regards to appropriate rules (compliance), incentive systems, control, and sanction mechanisms, setting, clarifying and fairly applying standards for performance, and formulating appropriate expectations, recruiting, promoting and developing staff, organizing information exchange, communication and reflection, providing support in conflict situations, and especially by avoiding (relevant) inconsistencies (between rules, promises, and values).

3.3.4 Role model

Finally, good leadership invests in trust by acting as a role model.
While establishing norms, rules, and systems that foster the conditions for GVT members to invest accordingly into the ethical focal point, do no (illegitimate) harm for trust, GVL is advised to stick to the elaborated norms, rules, and systems itself to demonstrate its trustworthiness (cf. 3.2.3). Furthermore, GVL can demonstrate trustworthy behavior by showing (self-) commitment, integrity, by avoiding relevant inconsistencies—and showing self-restraint (cf. 3.2.3). GVL can thus introduce token of trustworthiness and reliability of its behavior which can, in turn, serve as the basis for the willingness of team members to make specific investments in line with the ethical focal point do no (illegitimate) harm (Suchanek, 2010, p. 284).

A good leader-follower relationship is crucial for trust in a virtual context and requires GVL to lead by example while empowering its members to be responsible self-leaders (Flavian et al., 2019; Jawadi, 2013; Norman et al., 2019). According to prior GVT research, virtual leadership traits and competencies for trust are GVL's communication competencies, integrity, honesty, openness, relationships both inside and outside of work, the leader's professional competence, knowledge, abilities, intelligence, and experience, and most importantly the 'congruence' between espoused and enacted values (Norman et al., 2019, p. 290). This 'congruence' is in line with leadership ethics literature which emphasizes the importance of aligning words and actions for trust (Suchanek & von Broock, 2008).

Thus, GVL is recommended to self-commit to this proposed model of good leadership for trust in teams with regards to 1) the attitude of respect towards all GVT members, 2) the creation of and the complying with a shared (team) mental model of (illegitimate) harm in GVTs, 3) setting up framework conditions in line with the ethical focal point do no (illegitimate) harm and complying with these conditions 4) by acting as a role model through its own behavior (Suchanek, 2019). Thus, leadership's self-commitment to realize do no (illegitimate) harm is one of the most elementary foundations of successful and responsible leadership. The importance lies in the consistency of these points, which creates reliability and ultimately engenders trust.

Thus, in its role as an active e-trust promoter good and successful GVL acts as a role model concerning the above-elaborated framework of good leadership for trust while further demonstrating trustworthy behavior to inspire GVT members to invest accordingly into the ethical focal point do no (illegitimate) harm by aligning words and actions while showing (self-) commitment, integrity, avoiding relevant inconsistencies and showing self-restraint.

Overall, this subchapter has answered the research question of how GVL can actively promote trust and create common ground regarding mutual reliable trust expectations in socio-culturally diverse GVTs. The point of this thesis is that in its role as an active e-trust promoter, good and successful GVL can create trust in GVTs by investing itself into trust by realizing the ethical focal point do no (illegitimate) harm alongside the good leadership model (2019) and its four orientations.

Moreover, this thesis has enriched the definition of GVL's role as an e-trust promoter (Fajen, 2018, p. 319). It has shown that in line with the fact that realizing trust in GVT is the major challenge for GVL, GVL's role as an e-trust promoter entails many different roles and tasks that are equally challenging and require GVL to have specific virtual leadership competencies and personality traits. The role of an active e-trust promoter entails all the other roles such as the roles of e-node, e-networker, e-organizer, e-coordinator, e-motivator, e-supporter, e-developer, e-controller, e-decision maker, e-responsible person and e-communicator as categorized by Fajen (2018). GVL's role as an e-trust promoter is thus the most challenging and encompassing of all roles. Therefore, the role of an e-trust promoter requires GVL to make investments to fulfill its function and to create trust in GVT for effective cooperation and enhanced performance.

3.4 Illustration Case of Global Virtual Leadership Realizing Do No (Illegitimate) Harm

This thesis has applied some elements of the above-mentioned business ethical model of good leadership in a tailor-made leadership development program created explicitly for the global virtual organization Think-it (Avantgardist Institut, 2021). In line with the analyses mentioned above and the consequent merger of GVT research and business ethics literature, this case illustration offers specific training to enhance SMM similarity (cf. 3.3.3) for Think-it members and its leaders concerning the illegitimacy harm by raising awareness of the basis of trustful cooperation in GVTs through team interaction, reflection, exercises, and discussion.

3.4.1 Case Illustration Overview

Think-it is an engineering collective on a mission to unlock human potential through the sustainable use of technology. Their high-tech and low-carbon solutions help innovative teams worldwide to lower costs, democratize data, and reach net-zero faster. With a focus on digital transformation, smart cloud-data infrastructure, and the UN SDGs, Think-it tackles significant problems that can only be solved with future-proof technology. The team members are experts in Software Engineering, Machine Learning, and DevOps & Cloud, and their global R&D network and unique approach to continuous learning allow them to grasp and use the newest technologies quickly, providing high-quality products for clients like BMW, SoundCloud, and XPrize (Think-it, 2022).

Founded in 2017, Think-it comprises a globally dispersed and diverse team based mainly in Germany, Northern Africa, and other countries, including 10 + nationalities and 35% of women. Think-it members and leaders work in a virtual setting with each other and their respective clients with little to no face-to-face contact. Team composition and structure rotate based on the clients' needs. Generally, teams are composed of three to five Think-iteers[53] who are supposed to complete specific software-related projects together. As Think-iteers work project-based in various constellations following requirements of a respective client, Think-it's members must be able to quickly adapt to the diverse and changing team composition and environment while accomplishing their projects on time. Moreover, Think-it's team has been steadily growing over the past five years since the company's creation. Nearly all members are hired online through virtual interviews with the founders, the HR department, and potentially some team members. Thus, Think-it's team members are supposed to be independent, have good forward thinking and problem-solving skills, and take responsibility for their work while having the confidence to admit mistakes and work as a team within company guidelines.

[53] Refers to Think-it's team members.

As identified in numerous interviews with the founders and respective leaders of Think-it, the central leadership challenge relates to trust. The rapid growth and constant hire of new people while working in a virtual context for 3rd parties is particularly challenging, superseded by the lack of face-to-face contact. Thus, the main challenge is building trust within a socio-culturally diverse and virtual environment. The lack of trust results in various issues concerning communication within the team. Founder Joscha Raue elucidates that Think-it is committed to a continuous open feedback culture. He would like to promote proactive and constructive communication and feedback in the company to tackle personal and professional issues. However, due to the diverse socio-cultural nature of the members and the absence of face-to-face encounters, feedback can be misunderstood and seen without positive intent but be misinterpreted as negativity or even insult. This engenders mistrust hindering effective collaboration and performance, and the question therefore arises:

– How can team leaders create trust-based relationships with new team members or clients already in the on-boarding phase?

– How can team leaders create trust within the team if so many new socio-culturally diverse members join in a short time? How can team leaders take the fear out of the equation?

– How can team leaders and members get comfortable with giving and receiving constructive feedback or addressing complex topics without hurting others or being hurt?

– How can team leaders and members assume positive intent from others within the feedback loop?

3.4.2 Do No (illegitimate) Harm Incorporated in a Tailor-Made Online Workshop

Think-it's leaders would like to incorporate their core values of collectivism, ownership, and trust as given in their mission statement in communication and actions. Thus, they would like to integrate them into the on-boarding framework for new team members and partners alike to promote trust. They would like to act as role models and first-movers and show their willingness to build trust by elaborating a framework that aims to establish a shared teamwork mental model regarding communication and constructive feedback proven to further effective collaboration.

As of that, this thesis research team and Think-it leaders joined forces and co-created a framework that incorporates the research of this thesis regarding the business ethical concept of the golden rule and its do no harm dimension. A tailor-made virtual three-day seminar followed by a one-month integration period with weekly check-ins for 36 Think-it members and leaders was created and executed from June to July 2021. Out of the 36 participants, six have been identified as team leaders and/or co-founders.

First, the main problem in the organization Think-it was identified with regards to trust in open and constructive communication and feedback in 1-1 and 1-many interviews with the founders and respective leaders of the company.

Second, after elaborating on the problem, an *introduction letter* and a *summary* of the project, as well as a presentation of this thesis research team, were sent to all participants. The main problem of constructive feedback and communication hindering trust-building in GVTs regarding socio-cultural distance and the dimensions of dispersion were elucidated. Furthermore, the following steps with regards to the creation of a tailor-made seminar were stated. As of that, a call for participation and open sharing of thoughts regarding trust and open and constructive communication and feedback was brought forward, preparing the participants to open up and share their issues within the company.

Third, Think-it leaders and this thesis research team have elaborated a detailed *questionnaire* regarding what hinders and affects trust-building and constructive feedback in their company which was sent to all participants. The questionnaire was answered anonymously, and the resulting answers were bundled and synthesized by Think-it leaders to reduce complexity. The answers supported the further deconstruction of the main problem while allowing this thesis research team to better grasp the mood within the company concerning trust and feedback.

Fourth, a *skills pre-assessment* was sent to all participants of the seminar. The pre-assessment measures each participant's skills regarding their collaboration capacity, perspective coordination, contextual thinking, and decision-making capacity. The skills matrix is based on the VUCA Leadership framework as elaborated by the research center and skill development organization Lectica Institute (Lectica, 2022). The VUCA skills are defined as meta-skills further divided into the matrix consisting of four broad mega-skills, namely (1) collaboration capacity, (2) perspective coordination, (3) contextual thinking, and (4) decision-making capacity.

Collaborative capacity skills refer to the ability "to work cooperatively with others in a variety of contexts, including collaborative learning, creative thinking, problem-solving, and decision-making" (Dawson, 2020a). These skills are considered "the most foundational of all VUCA skills, in that they either support the development of other VUCA skills or are called upon when practicing other VUCA skills. Collaborative capacity skills include self-regulation, perspective-seeking, perspective-taking, and communication." (Dawson, 2020).

"Perspective-coordination skills build upon and increase collaborative capacity skills. They are essential for constructing knowledge, resolving conflicts, and making decisions. Thus, they support human interactions by fostering mutual Respect, nurturing creativity, expanding minds, generating and developing ideas, leveraging conflict, and supporting healthy relationships" (Dawson, 2021).

Contextual thinking skills leverage and extend collaborative capacity and perspective coordination skills. They are essential for constructing knowledge, solving problems, and making decisions—especially in complex situations. Their development is explicitly connected to the mental complexity of an individual. Contextual thinking involves a set of complementary skills that increase the scope, depth, and accuracy of understanding issues, problems, or conflicts (Dawson, 2021).

"Decision-making process skills leverage and extend collaborative capacity, perspective coordination, and contextual thinking skills. They are essential for addressing conflicts, solving problems, and making decisions—especially in complex situations." (Dawson, 2021)

All four mega skills are further deconstructed into macro, micro, and mini skills. From a learning perspective, mini and micro-skills are most relevant because they can be practiced in context and in real-time, which allows for building the mega skills over time. The pre-assessment aims to find out where each participant stands regarding their micro and mini skills. The pre-assessment is based on self- and other assessments where differences in perspectives can be tracked.

Fifth, based on the open questionnaire and the skills pre-assessment, a tailor-made three-day virtual seminar for Think-iteers was elaborated. The seminar was organized on the video conference software *zoom*. Moreover, *google docs* were used to track group exercises and to put participants in pairs for a buddy program, while the open chart program *mentimenter* was used to gather opinions on specific questions. A hand-out with all relevant information and content of the course with exercises was shared with the participants after each seminar day.

The seminar's title is "How to give and receive constructive feedback & communication? Become an intrapreneur through the empowerment of 21st-century VUCA Leadership Skills." As Think-it is committed to a continuous open feedback culture, the seminar supports its members to develop the right mindset to work in GVTs in a fast-paced, ever-changing environment while enhancing their communication skills.

The seminar aimed to build Think-it's members' intrapreneurial mindset through empowering 21st-century VUCA Leadership skills. Participants were further given academic and practical input with tools to train related mini and micro skills related to each building block of each day. The seminar is structured based on the following three modules: (1) self-awareness, (2) self-leadership, and (3) trustful cooperation The seminar bridges the gap between academic inputs concerning business ethics, neuroscience, psychology, and related subjects, further elucidating the New Work Challenges of GVTs while teaching practical tools and techniques such as breath work, meditation, and non-violent communication allowing to give and receive constructive feedback with the overall aim to build trust.

Academic input was given by this thesis doctoral supervisors Prof. Dr. Suchanek (HHL) and Prof. Dr. Dauth (HHL), with regards to their respective research topics, namely business ethics (Suchanek) and the concept of respect and do no (illegitimate) harm and an introduction about New Work and associated challenges in the global virtual environment (Dauth). Furthermore, academic input was given by this thesis author Dr. Lili Jassemi regarding self-awareness, self-leadership, trust, and cooperation. Expert practitioners Dr. Felix Wittke, Antimo Di Donato, and Eva Kaczor brought practical wisdom in the form of tools, techniques, and coaching.

Divided into 1) self-awareness, 2) self-leadership, and 3) trustful cooperation, each seminar module was followed by a one-hour to two practice session where the course content regarding the practical tools and techniques were deepened while leaving space for further comments and questions.

Moreover, the seminar was built on Think-it's real teams' contexts as participants were asked to prepare real-life challenges concerning miscommunication and harm, further discussed in break-out sessions and the whole group. The seminar additionally offered a buddy program with a learning journal, team learning, and leadership development based on the VUCA skills matrix with performance tracking.

Regarding the program, the first module (1) self-awareness laid down the basics of do no (illegitimate) harm in teams, starting at the individual level. Teachings about being aware of one's actions, reactions, and blind spots were brought forward. Practical exercises underpinned this content to create space for reflection and introspection.

The second module, (2) self-leadership, explored the importance of leading oneself in a global virtual environment as the basis to realize do no (illegitimate) harm. Prof. Dr. Suchanek gave an in-depth analysis of the golden rule and its do no harm dimension with special regard to the concept of respect. Several group exercises and open discussions concerning respect and harm were executed during this module, aiming to lay down the various perspectives within the team concerning respect and harm. All results were summarized on *google docs* and the group chat, which was sent in the aftermath to all participants, preparing them for the following practice session. Participants were asked to analyze one specific example from their professional context regarding harm and disrespect in communication and feedback. Self and buddy commitment regarding how not to harm others were identified for each participant and shared openly in the chat and the group discussion.

The third module (3), trustful cooperation, offered a summary of the findings while elaborating a joint framework of how respectful communication and feedback should look in Think-its team context. As of that, practices and communication rules were elaborated by the participants in small groups and shared and stored on google docs for further discussion. Practices of non-violent communication and active listening techniques were brought forward and practiced in break-out sessions with the suitable elaborated methods for giving feedback aforementioned elaborated by the participants.

The course structure followed the practical syllogism's business ethical heuristical investment tool in the respective three modules. The first module *(1), self-awareness,* lays down what Think-it's team aims for: building trust based on constructive communication and feedback. The second module *(2), self-leadership,* explored the real-life challenges regarding trust and feedback in the team, where various perspectives of respect and harm concerning communication were openly discussed. Finally, the third module *(3), trustful cooperation,* laid down how good and respective communication and feedback should be given in the team to fulfill the goal. Thus, relevant good practices and rules for communication were elaborated and underpinned by training.

The aim of this pilot project was to get the different perspectives of harm regarding communication and feedback in the company and display it for everybody to see and discuss. The participants further elaborated with their leaders and this thesis research team what a shared (team) mental model of harm could look like. However, the elaboration of such a model was outside the seminar's scope.

3.4.3 Outcome

The overall outcome of the seminar and integration sessions was very successful, with a dedicated two-hour feedback sessions from participants for this thesis research team. Feedback included what ways the seminar could be improved.

The participants said they would have appreciated having more real-life examples from the software engineering context while having more time to discuss in break-out sessions. They also noted that the program was very dense and would have preferred less input but more practice.

Positive feedback was given with regards to the overall structure of the course, the course content, and the relevance for Think-it's context. Participants agreed that the content was communicated well by all teachers and coaches. The lecturers' didactics and capacities to answer the participants' questions were highly appreciated and recognized, which led to overall high satisfaction with the course.

Think-it's founders and leaders organized an internal feedback session with this thesis research team. They stated that during the month of the course, they reached the highest score regarding overall team satisfaction and cohesion since the beginning of the company's creation in 2017. Think-it's leaders regularly send out polls to measure team motivation and satisfaction. Furthermore, Think-it and the research team of this thesis will, in a subsequent step, refine the given seminar and co-create a global virtual leadership course for the software realm specifically.

Conclusion

4

4.1 Research Summary

GVTs are growing in importance and popularity as they maintain the increasingly globalized social and economic infrastructure while offering various benefits for companies and employees alike (cf. 2.2.1). The employment of GVTs has been accelerated due to the COVID-19 crisis since the first quarter of 2020. Ever since organizations that offer remote work policies which combine virtual and mixed forms of virtual teamwork have been on the rise (cf. 2.2.1). Virtual work is one of the biggest drivers of the transformation of the workplace (Powers, 2018, p. 7). The successful employment of GVTs is thus one of the most critical future entrepreneurial challenges, and organizations that do not use GVTs effectively may not be able to survive in a global, competitive, and rapidly changing environment (Duarte & Snyder, 2006, p. 4). Marked by spatial, temporal, and structural dispersion of its members, GVTs encounter a multitude of challenges related to communication, the use of technology, and socio-cultural differences (cf. 2.2.2). Thus, GVTs often fail to perform and cooperate effectively due to miscommunication and misunderstandings leading to various types of conflicts which undermines the creation trust (cf. 2.2.3).

This thesis has shown that adequate GVL is indispensable to unfold the full potential of GVTs for effective cooperation and performance (cf. 2.3.1, cf. 2.3.2, cf. 3.3). As of that, GVL must have a specific understanding of how to properly guide and lead digitally socio-culturally diverse people (cf. 2.3.2, cf. 2.3.3, cf. 3.3) while diffusing conflicts and finding comprises between all members to ensure team performance (cf. 3.2.3). Performance is based on successful interactions between GVT members and trust is a fundamental condition for effective collaboration (cf. 3.1.1). Even though the creation of trust in GVTs has been pointed

L. Jassemi, *Global Virtual Teams & Trust*, Gabler Theses,
https://doi.org/10.1007/978-3-658-41852-6_4

out as the main challenge for GVL (cf. 2.3.1), it is also the most important task of GVL to lead effectively.

Thus, GVL needs to find levers to cope with the negative effects of virtuality and socio-cultural distance to create and sustain trust to ensure GVT performance (Jawadi, 2013). Even though prior GVT research provides valuable insights into trust in GVTs, it has not elucidated what concrete actions and tools GVL can use to actively promote the formation of mutual trust expectations in socio-cultural diverse GVTs (cf. 2.4).

Thus, this thesis has proposed the research question: How can GVL actively promote trust in socio-culturally diverse GVTs and form mutual trust expectations that ultimately lead to effective cooperation and performance?

This dissertation has filled this research gap and answered the research question by introducing a business ethical perspective on trust in teams while merging key findings on trust, GVTs, and GVL. It has further applied the heuristical tool of the practical syllogism to merge values and reality to derive adequate actions. The point of this thesis is that in its role as an active e-trust promoter good and successful GVL can create trust in GVTs by investing itself into trust by realizing the ethical focal point do no (illegitimate) harm (cf. 3.3). GVL can do so by applying the business ethical model of good leadership for trust (Suchanek, 2019) which offers points of orientation for its behavior as well as for GVT members alongside the following four dimensions: showing respect to GVT members (3.3.1), providing a frame of orientation by creating an SMM of (illegitimate) harm (3.3.2), setting framework conditions for trust (3.3.3) and acting as a role model through trustworthy behavior while showing consistency in communication and actions (3.3.4).

4.2 Research Contributions

This dissertation has brought business ethical concepts to the overall study of leadership and trust in GVTs and has successfully underpinned these with prior key GVT findings. This thesis offers five contributions to GVT literature and business ethics that will be summarized in the following.

First, this thesis contributes to GVT literature by introducing the *business ethical concept of the ethical focal point do no (illegitimate harm) for trust* (cf. 3.1.2, 3.1.3). The golden rule's do no harm principle has been elucidated as the central and necessary condition for trust in (global virtual) teams for long-term social cooperation (cf. 3.1.2, cf. 3.1.3). Moreover, the ethical focal point do no (illegitimate) harm has been introduced as the primary point of orientation to align respective trust expectations and actions in (global virtual) teams (Suchanek & Entschew, 2018). It has been shown that the ethical focal point. do no illegitimate harm can serve as common ground for trust in GVTs (cf. 3.1.3). Thus, the first contribution of this thesis is the introduction of a new conceptual model which allows a better understanding of the trust creation process in general, which can be applied to GVTs while offering GVL points of orientation for actions and expectations that create trust in teams.

Second, this thesis contributes to new knowledge with regards to research on SMM in GVTs and, more particularly, on *shared mental model similarity* (J. Schmidtke & Cummings, 2017) by proposing the ethical focal point do no (illegitimate) harm as SMM to align trust expectations and actions in GVTs (cf. 3.2.2). To fulfill its function as an (ethical) focal point and be similar enough to align individual MMs (the illegitimacy of) harm needs to be a shared understanding between all GVT members (cf. 3.2.1, cf. 3.2.2). As an example of common ground, SMMs are of the utmost importance in GVTs for effective cooperation. The importance of a shared understanding of harm for trust is further highlighted in GVTs due to socio-cultural differences that impact the respective interpretations of the (illegitimacy) harm which in turn forms trust expectations and ultimately affects performance (cf. 3.2.1, cf. 3.2.2). As an example of common ground, SMMs are of the utmost importance in GVTs for effective cooperation. According to SMM research, a working SMM needs a critical overlap of certain information to be concurrent or similar enough (Converse et al., 1993). Thus, the second contribution of this thesis is the introduction of the ethical focal point do no (illegitimate) harm as common ground for trust, if it is a shared understanding between all stakeholders in GVTs involved forming a working shared (team) mental model to form mutual trust expectations.

Third, this thesis contributes new knowledge by introducing the heuristical model of the *practical syllogism* as a tool to merge normative and empirical levels concerning trust in GVTs. The three interrelated orders of this tool convey ethics and realism and allow to derive relevant courses of action and expectations (Suchanek, 2015, pp. 41–53). While the first order (cf. 3.1) relates to the normative value of leading effective GVTs based on trust (cf. 3.1), the second order (cf. 3.2) relates to the empirical reality of trust-building in GVTs and has summarized the challenges concerning the formation of mutual trust expectations and underpinned GVL's role in building trust in GVTs. The third and last order represents the reconciliation between the first and second order and results in what GVL should to achieve the first order, namely leading effective GVTs based on trust (cf. 3.1). Thus, the third contribution of this thesis is the introduction of a new tool that balances values and reality with regards to trust building in GVTs to bring about practical implementation advice for GVL to realize trust given the conditions and challenges of reality.

Fourth, this thesis contributes to new knowledge by introducing the *model of good leadership* for trust in teams (Suchanek, 2019) and applying it to a real *illustration case* for the company Think-it. Conceptually, this model has been applied as the third order of the practical syllogism to derive actions and expectations for trust in teams (cf. 3.3). Additionally, the illustration case refers to a tailor-made three-day seminar followed by a one month of integration session for 36 GVT members including six leaders (cf. 3.4). Some core elements of that model with regards to do no (illegitimate) harm have been integrated to refine the understanding of the illegitimacy of harm in the company by merging various tools like individual and team reflection, playful interactions, and interactive exercises as well as content-driven lectures with Prof. Dr. Suchanek and Prof. Dr. Dauth as well as expert practitioners. Thus, this thesis has contributed new knowledge by offering a novel perspective and a practical tool to implement trust in socio-culturally diverse GVTs with a step-by-step guideline concerning actions and expectations for GVL, especially regarding GVL's behavior and attitude.

Finally, this thesis has enriched the definition of GVL's role as an active e-trust promoter (Fajen, 2018, p. 319) by offering a detailed count of tasks, attitudes, and behavior that GVL should realize to demonstrate its trustworthiness, which is key to create trust in GVTs (cf. 3.2.3; cf. 3.3). It has been shown that GVL not only needs to have specific virtual leadership competencies and personality traits (cf. 2.3.3) but that the role of an e-trust promoter entails all the other roles above such as the roles of e-node, e-networker, e-organizer, e-coordinator, e-motivator, e-supporter, e-developer, e-controller, e-decision maker, e-responsible person, and e-communicator as categorized by Fajen (2018) (cf. 2.3.2). Thus, this thesis has shown that GVL's role of an active e-trust promoter requires GVL to invest into trust to create trust in GVTs for effective cooperation and team performance. This thesis found this to be the most challenging but rewarding and all-encompassing of all roles.

4.3 Research Limitations

Regarding research limitations, this thesis did not elucidate GVTs, GVL, and trust research related to COVID-19. Since the emergence of the global pandemic, GVTs have seen a massive rise overnight due to the lack of other options and the necessity to keep the social and economic infrastructure running. The trust-building process in GVTs that have worked together previously face-to-face and that have a long-standing history of working together might be very different than in the case of GVTs in this thesis that, per definition, do not meet face-to-face or at least very seldom. Further research on the impact of COVID-19 on trust in GVTs is needed, and how these new findings may change this thesis's conclusions or not.

Moreover, this thesis has only researched trust as ethical value and its impact on cooperation and performance in GVTs. It did not elaborate on other ethical values such as fairness or kindness. Other ethical values that could serve as focal points to align expectations and actions for team performance should thus be further inquired about in GVT research.

Additionally, this thesis focused on what GVL can actively do to promote trust in GVTs. Other relevant stakeholders such as third parties that could potentially influence trust in GVTs like governments or clients are not considered. Thus, further research concerning the trust creation process in GVTs is needed concerning other stakeholders involved. Moreover, this thesis is a solely conceptual work with one case illustration. Thus, empirical research regarding business ethical models and contributions needs further study and validity.

Finally, the concept of *global* virtual teams has been meticulously defined and deconstructed into the dimensions of multicultural, culture, diversity, and socio-cultural distance in this thesis. However, GVT research needs more nuanced definitions of the concept of global and its underlying dimensions. Most VT research does not even differentiate between global virtual teams or solely virtual teams, as it presupposes that virtual teams are mostly globally dispersed and that they are, per definition, composed of different cultures. However, as this dissertation has shown, socio-cultural distance factors highly impact team effectivity and performance and should not be disregarded or intertwined with other concepts to undertake severe and adequate academic research.

4.4 Research Outlook

Especially with regards to socio-cultural distance and the formation of trust in a virtual context, more detailed research is needed. Research should look into the trust formation process regarding socio-culturally diverse members and take the dimensions of time, experience, knowledge, and character amongst others under further scrutiny to provide a more holistic view of the formation of trust expectations.

Employing GVTs as a new organizational structure is spreading rapidly within the corporate, public, and private sectors. This new form of cooperation is *digital, diverse, and decentralized.* To function, GVTs need substantial cooperation based on trust between their members to ensure team performance. Thus, this thesis has inspired the creation of Avantgardist Institut, a research and educational platform embedded in a community that promotes *3D Cooperation & Leadership: digital, diverse, and decentralized* (Avantgardist Institut, 2021). The case illustration of this thesis is based on the company Think-it represents the first leadership seminar and pilot project of Avantgardist Institut. By merging academic research and practical wisdom, Avantgardist Institut aims to respond to the needs of virtual teams and leaders and support them in overcoming the communication challenges as described in this thesis. Avantgardist Institut aims to provide virtual and actual co-learning, co-working, and co-creation spaces based on the core values of trust, inclusion, and co-creation to respond to the changing economic, social, and political environment of the 21st century.

References

Acs, Z. J., & Preston, L. (1997). Small and medium-sized enterprises, technology, and globalization: Introduction to a special issue on small and medium-sized enterprises in the global economy. *Small Business Economics*, *9*(1), 1–6.

Agerfalk, P. J., Fitzgerald, B., Holmstrom Olsson, H., Lings, B., Lundell, B., & Ó Conchúir, E. (2005). A framework for considering opportunities and threats in distributed software development. *In Proceedings of the International Workshop on Distributed Software Development*.

Alderfer, C. P. (1977). Group and Intergroup Relations. *Hackman JR, Suttle JL.: Improving Life at Work: Behavioral Science Approaches to Organizational Change, Santa Monica, CA: Goodyear*.

Anthony, J. (2020, April 7). *70 Virtual Team Statistics You Can't Ignore: 2021/2022 Data Analysis, Benefits & Challenges*. Financesonline.Com. https://financesonline.com/virtual-team-statistics/

Antoni, C. H. (2000). *Teamarbeit gestalten*. Beltz.

Armstrong, D. J., & Cole, P. (1995). Managing distances and differences in geographically distributed work groups. In *Diversity in work teams: Research paradigms for a changing workplace* (pp. 187–215). American Psychological Association.

Avantgardist Institut. (2021). *Think-it Leadership Development Program*. www.avantgardistinstitut.com

Badaracco, J., & Ellsworth, R. R. (1989). *Leadership and the Quest for Integrity*. Harvard Business Press.

Balliet, D., & Van Lange, P. A. (2013). Trust, conflict, and cooperation: A meta-analysis. *Psychological Bulletin, 139*(5), 1090.

Batarseh, F. S., Usher, J. M., & Daspit, J. J. (2017). Collaboration Capability in virtual Teams: Examining the Influence on Diversity and Innovation. *International Journal of Innovation Management*, *21*(04), 1750034.

Battin, R. D., Crocker, R., Kreidler, J., & Subramanian, K. (2001). Leveraging resources in global software development. *IEEE Software*, *18*(2), 70–77.

Ben-Ner, A., & Halldorsson, F. (2010). Trusting and trustworthiness: What are they, how to measure them, and what affects them. *Journal of Economic Psychology*, *31*(1), 64–79.

Bergiel, B. J., Bergiel, E. B., & Balsmeier, P. W. (2008). Nature of virtual teams: A summary of their advantages and disadvantages. *Management Research News*, *31*(2), 99–110.

L. Jassemi, *Global Virtual Teams & Trust*, Gabler Theses,
https://doi.org/10.1007/978-3-658-41852-6

Bjørn, P., Esbensen, M., Jensen, R. E., & Matthiesen, S. (2014). Does Distance Still Matter? Revisiting the CSCW Fundamentals on Distributed Collaboration. *ACM Transactions on Computer-Human Interaction, 21*(5), 1–26. https://doi.org/https://doi.org/10.1145/2670534

Bowles, S. (2016). *The moral economy: Why good incentives are no substitute for good citizens*. Yale University Press.

Breuer, C., Hüffmeier, J., & Hertel, G. (2016). Does trust matter more in virtual teams? A meta-analysis of trust and team effectiveness considering virtuality and documentation as moderators. *Journal of Applied Psychology, 101*(8), 1151–1177.

Burke, C. S., Sims, D. E., Lazzara, E. H., & Salas, E. (2007). Trust in leadership: A multi-level review and integration. *The Leadership Quarterly, 18*(6), 606–632.

Burns, J. M. (2012). *Leadership*. Open Road Media.

Calefato, F., & Lanubile, F. (2018). Establishing personal trust-based connections in distributed teams. *Internet Technology Letters, 1*(4), e6.

Cambridge Dictionary, D. (2014). *COMMITMENT | Bedeutung im Cambridge Englisch Wörterbuch*. https://dictionary.cambridge.org/de/worterbuch/englisch/commitment

Carson, T. L. (2003). Self–interest and business ethics: Some lessons of the recent corporate scandals. *Journal of Business Ethics, 43*(4), 389–394.

Cascio, W. F. (2000). Managing a virtual workplace. *Academy of Management Perspectives, 14*(3), 81–90.

Cheng, X., Yin, G., Azadegan, A., & Kolfschoten, G. (2016). Trust Evolvement in Hybrid Team Collaboration: A Longitudinal Case Study. *Group Decision and Negotiation, 25*(2), 267–288.

Cho, J. (2006). The mechanism of trust and distrust formation and their relational outcomes. *Journal of Retailing, 82*(1), 25–35.

Choi, O.-K., & Cho, E. (2019). The mechanism of trust affecting collaboration in virtual teams and the moderating roles of the culture of autonomy and task complexity. *Computers in Human Behavior, 91*, 305–315.

Clark, H. (1996). *Using Language*. Cambridge University Press.

Clark, H. H., & Brennan, S. E. (1991). Grounding in communication. In L. B. Resnick, J. M. Levine, & S. D. Teasley (Eds.), *Perspectives on socially shared cognition*. (pp. 127–149). American Psychological Association. https://doi.org/10.1037/10096-006

Colquitt, J., Scott, B. A., & Lepine, J. (2007). Trust, trustworthiness, and trust propensity: A meta-analytic test of their unique relationships with risk taking and job performance. *The Journal of Applied Psychology*. https://www.ocf.berkeley.edu/~reetaban/triple%20helix/trust%20and%20decision%20making.pdf

Converse, S., Cannon-Bowers, J., & Salas, E. (1993). Shared mental models in expert team decision making. *Individual and Group Decision Making: Current Issues, 221*, 221–246.

Cramton, C. D. (2001). The Mutual Knowledge Problem and Its Consequences for Dispersed Collaboration. *Organization Science, 12*(3), 346–371.

Crisp, C. B., & Jarvenpaa, S. L. (2013). Swift Trust in Global Virtual Teams. *Journal of Personnel Psychology, 12*(1), 45–56.

Cummings, J. N. (2011). Geography is alive and well in virtual teams. *Communications of the ACM, 54*(8), 24–26. https://doi.org/https://doi.org/10.1145/1978542.1978551

Cummings, J. N., & Kiesler, S. (2005). Collaborative Research Across Disciplinary and Organizational Boundaries. *Social Studies of Science, 35*(5), 703–722.

Cundill, G., Harvey, B., Tebboth, M., Cochrane, L., Currie-Alder, B., Vincent, K., Lawn, J., Nicholls, Robert. J., Scodanibbio, L., Prakash, A., New, M., Wester, P., Leone, M., Morchain, D., Ludi, E., DeMaria-Kinney, J., Khan, A., & Landry, M.-E. (2019). Large-Scale Transdisciplinary Collaboration for Adaptation Research: Challenges and Insights. *Global Challenges*, *3*(4), 1700132.

Curşeu, P. (2006). Emergent States in Virtual Teams: A Complex Adaptive Systems Perspective. *Journal of Information Technology*, *21*, 249–261.

Daassi, M., Jawadi, N., Favier, M., & Kalika, M. (2010). Building collective awareness in virtual teams: The effect of leadership behavioral style. In *Leadership in the Digital Enterprise: Issues and Challenges* (pp. 105–117). IGI Global.

Dawson, T. (2020). *VUCA unpacked (2)—Collaborative capacity* | [Medium]. https://theo-dawson.medium.com/vuca-unpacked-2-collaborative-capacity-4d794378dd25

Dawson, T. (2021a, January 31). VUCA unpacked (3)—Perspective coordination. *Medium*. https://theo-dawson.medium.com/vuca-unpacked-3-perspective-coordination-13e722981ce6

Dawson, T. (2021b, January 31). VUCA unpacked (5)—Decision-making process. *Medium*. https://theo-dawson.medium.com/vuca-unpacked-5-decision-making-process-db0c1493f190

Dawson, T. (2021c, February 11). VUCA unpacked (4)—Contextual thinking. *Medium*. https://theo-dawson.medium.com/vuca-unpacked-4-contextual-thinking-a5baaecfb270

De Biasi, K. (2019). *Solving the Change Paradox by Means of Trust*. Wiesbaden. Springer.

De Jong, B. A., Dirks, K. T., & Gillespie, N. (2016). Trust and team performance: A meta-analysis of main effects, moderators, and covariates. *Journal of Applied Psychology*, *101*(8), 1134–1150.

Dekker, D. M., Rutte, C. G., & Van den Berg, P. T. (2008). Cultural differences in the perception of critical interaction behaviors in global virtual teams. *International Journal of Intercultural Relations*, *32*(5), 441–452.

Dennis, Fuller, & Valacich. (2008). Media, Tasks, and Communication Processes: A Theory of Media Synchronicity. *MIS Quarterly*, *32*(3), 575.

DeRosa, D. M., Hantula, D. A., Kock, N., & D'Arcy, J. (2004). Trust and leadership in virtual teamwork: A media naturalness perspective. *Human Resource Management: Published in Cooperation with the School of Business Administration, The University of Michigan and in Alliance with the Society of Human Resources Management*, *43*(2-3), 219–232.

Deutsch, M. (1958). Trust and suspicion. *Journal of Conflict Resolution*, *2*(4), 265–279.

Diehl, E., & Sterman, J. D. (1995). Effects of feedback complexity on dynamic decision making. *Organizational Behavior and Human Decision Processes*, *62*(2), 198–215.

Dourish, P., & Bellotti, V. (1992). *Awareness and coordination in shared workspaces*. 107–114.

Drucker, P. (1986). *The Frontiers of Management: Where Tomorrow's Decisions Are Being Shaped Today by Drucker, Peter F.: Fine Hardcover (1986) 1st Edition | 2nd Act Media.*

Druskat, V. U., & Pescosolido, A. T. (2002). The content of effective teamwork mental models in self-managing teams: Ownership, learning and heedful interrelating. *Human Relations*, *55*(3), 283–314.

Duarte, D., & Tennant, N. (1999). Mastering Virtual Teams: Strategies, Tools, and Techniques That Succeed. In *Internet and Higher Education—INTERNET HIGH EDUC* (Vol. 3, p. 229).

Dubé, L., & Robey, D. (2009). Surviving the paradoxes of virtual teamwork. *Information Systems Journal*, *19*(1), 3–30.

Dubrovsky, V. J., Kiesler, S., & Sethna, B. N. (1991). The equalization phenomenon: Status effects in computer-mediated and face-to-face decision-making groups. *Human-Computer Interaction*, *6*(2), 119–146.

Durnell Cramton, C., & Hinds, P. J. (2004). Subgroup dynamics in internationally distributed teams: Ethnocentrism or cross-national learning? *Research in Organizational Behavior*, *26*, 231–263.

Earley, P. C., & Gibson, C. B. (2002). *Multinational work teams: A new perspective.* Routledge.

Edwards, H. K., & Sridhar, V. (2005). Analysis of Software Requirements Engineering Exercises in a Global Virtual Team Setup. *Journal of Global Information Management (JGIM)*, *13*(2), 21–41.

Espinosa, J. A., & Carmel, E. (2004). The effect of time separation on coordination costs in global software teams: A dyad model. *37th Annual Hawaii International Conference on System Sciences, 2004. Proceedings of The*, 10 pp.

Espinosa, J. A., & Pickering, C. (2006). The Effect of Time Separation on Coordination Processes and Outcomes: A Case Study. *Proceedings of the 39th Annual Hawaii International Conference on System Sciences (HICSS'06)*, 25b–25b.

Fajen, A. (2018). Führung multikultureller virtueller Teams als zentrale Herausforderung für Führungskräfte im 21. Jahrhundert. In *Erfolgreiche Führung multikultureller virtueller Teams* (pp. 1–21). Springer.

Fiol, C. M., & O'Connor, E. J. (2005). Identification in Face-to-Face, Hybrid, and Pure Virtual Teams: Untangling the Contradictions. *Organization Science*, *16*(1), 19–32.

Fjermestad, J. (2004). An analysis of communication mode in group support systems research. *Decision Support Systems*, *37*(2), 239–263.

Flavian, C., Guinalíu, M., & Jordan, P. (2019). Antecedents and consequences of trust on a virtual team leader. *European Journal of Management and Business Economics*, *28*(1), 2–24. https://doi.org/https://doi.org/10.1108/EJMBE-11-2017-0043

Flores, F., & Solomon, R. C. (1998). Creating Trust1. *Business Ethics Quarterly*, *8*(2), 205–232.

Ford, R. C., Piccolo, R. F., & Ford, L. R. (2017). Strategies for building effective virtual teams: Trust is key. *Business Horizons*, *60*(1), 25–34.

Fulmer, C. A., & Gelfand, M. J. (2012). At what level (and in whom) we trust: Trust across multiple organizational levels. *Journal of Management*, *38*(4), 1167–1230.

Gambetta, D. (1988). *Trust: Making and breaking cooperative relations.*

Gibson, C. B., & Cohen, S. G. (Eds.). (2003). *Virtual teams that work: Creating conditions for virtual team effectiveness* (1st ed). Jossey-Bass.

Gibson, C. B., & Gibbs, J. L. (2006). *Unpacking the Concept of Virtuality: The Effects of Geographic Dispersion, Electronic Dependence, Dynamic Structure, and National Diversity on Team Innovation.* 46.

Gibson, C. B., Huang, L., Kirkman, B. L., & Shapiro, D. L. (2014). Where global and virtual meet: The value of examining the intersection of these elements in twenty-first-century teams. *Annu. Rev. Organ. Psychol. Organ. Behav.*, *1*(1), 217–244.

Gibson, C. B., & Manuel, J. A. (2003). Building trust. *Virtual Teams That Work*, 59–86.

GitLab. (2020). *The Future of Work is Remote.* The Remote Work Report. https://about.gitlab.com/company/culture/all-remote/remote-work-report-2020/

Glikson, E., Woolley, A. W., Gupta, P., & Kim, Y. J. (2019). Visualized Automatic Feedback in Virtual Teams. *Frontiers in Psychology, 10.*

Gobeli, S., Spiegel-Steinmann, B., Rack, O., & Tschaut, A. (2012). *Anreizmanagement in virtuellen Teams-Erfolgreiche Strategien zur Motivation von Mitarbeitenden.*

Gunnthorsdottir, A., McCabe, K., & Smith, V. (2002). Using the Machiavellianism instrument to predict trustworthiness in a bargaining game. *Journal of Economic Psychology, 23*(1), 49–66.

Guzzo, R. A., & Dickson, M. W. (1996). Teams in organizations: Recent research on performance and effectiveness. *Annual Review of Psychology, 47*(1), 307–338.

Hacker, J., Johnson, M., Saunders, C., & Thayer, A. (2019). Trust in Virtual Teams: A Multidisciplinary Review and Integration. *Australasian Journal of Information Systems, 23.*

Hackman, R. (1987). The design of work teams. In *Hand- book of Organizational Behavior* (p. p.315–342). Lorsch, J. W., NJ: Prentice-Hall.

Herbsleb, J., Mockus, A., Finholt, T., & Grinter, R. (2000). *Distance, dependencies, and delay in a global collaboration.* 319–328.

Hertel, G., Geister, S., & Konradt, U. (2005). Managing virtual teams: A review of current empirical research. *Human Resource Management Review, 15*(1), 69–95.

Hertel, G., Konradt, U., & Orlikowski, B. (2004). Managing distance by interdependence: Goal setting, task interdependence, and team-based rewards in virtual teams. *European Journal of Work and Organizational Psychology, 13*(1), 1–28.

Hertel, G., Schroer, J., Batinic, B., & Naumann, S. (2008). Do shy people prefer to send e-mail?: Personality effects on communication media preferences in threatening and non-threatening situations. *Social Psychology, 39*(4), 231.

Hinds, P. J., & Bailey, D. E. (2003). Out of Sight, Out of Sync: Understanding Conflict in Distributed Teams. *Organization Science, 14*(6), 615–632.

Hinds, P. J., & Mortensen, M. (2005). Understanding Conflict in Geographically Distributed Teams: The Moderating Effects of Shared Identity, Shared Context, and Spontaneous Communication. *Organization Science, 3*(16), 290–307.

Hoch, J. E., & Kozlowski, S. W. J. (2014). Leading virtual teams: Hierarchical leadership, structural supports, and shared team leadership. *Journal of Applied Psychology, 99*(3), 390–403.

Hofstede, G. (1984). *Culture's Consequences: International Differences in Work-Related Values.* London. Sage.

Hofstede, G. (1993). *Interikulturelle zusammenarbeit.* Wiesbaden.Springer.

Hofstede, G. (2001). *Culture's consequences: Comparing values, behaviors, institutions, and organizations across nations.* London. Sage.

Hofstede, G. (2011). Dimensionalizing cultures: The Hofstede model in context. *Online Readings in Psychology and Culture, 2*(1), 2307–0919.

Hollander, E. P. (1978). *Leadership dynamics: A practical guide to effective relationships.* The Free Press.

Holmstrom Olsson, H., Ó Conchúir, E., Ågerfalk, P., & Fitzgerald, B. (2006). *Global Software Development Challenges: A Case Study on Temporal, Geographical and Socio-Cultural Distance.* 3–11.

Homann, K. (2014). *Karl Homann (2014): Sollen und Können. Grenzen und Bedingungen der Individualmoral, Wien: Ibera Verlag/European University Press Verlags GmbH.*

Hosmer, L. T. (1995). Trust: The connecting link between organizational theory and philosophical ethics. *Academy of Management Review, 20*(2), 379–403.

Hunsaker, P. L., & Hunsaker, J. S. (2008). Virtual teams: A leader's guide. *Team Performance Management: An International Journal.*

Jarvenpaa, S. L., & Leidner, D. E. (1999). Communication and Trust in Global Virtual Teams. *Organization Science, 10*(6), 791–815. https://doi.org/https://doi.org/10.1287/orsc.10.6.791

Jarvenpaa, S. L., Shaw, T. R., & Staples, D. S. (2004a). Toward Contextualized Theories of Trust: The Role of Trust in Global Virtual Teams. *Information Systems Research, 15*(3), 250–267.

Jawadi, N. (2013). E-leadership and trust management: Exploring the moderating effects of team virtuality. *International Journal of Technology and Human Interaction (IJTHI), 9*(3), 18–35.

Jehn, K. A. (1997). A Qualitative Analysis of Conflict Types and Dimensions in Organizational Groups. *Administrative Science Quarterly, 42*(3), 530–557.

Johnson, P., Heimann, V., & O'Neill, K. (2001). The "wonderland" of virtual teams. *Journal of Workplace Learning.*

Johnson, S., Bettenhausen, K., & Gibbons, E. (2009). Realities of Working in Virtual Teams: Affective and Attitudinal Outcomes of Using Computer-Mediated Communication. *Small Group Research—SMALL GROUP RES, 40.*

Johnson-Laird, P. N. (1989). *Mental models.*

Junea, P. (2015). *Virtual Team—Origin, Definition and its Scope.*

Jung, R. H., Bruck, J., & Quarg, S. (2011). Allgemeine Managementlehre. *Berlin.2011.*

Kanawattanachai, P., & Yoo, Y. (2002). Dynamic nature of trust in virtual teams. *The Journal of Strategic Information Systems, 11*(3), 187–213.

Kayworth, T. R., & Leidner, D. E. (2000). The global virtual manager: A prescription for success. *European Management Journal, 18*(2), 183–194.

Kayworth, T. R., & Leidner, D. E. (2002). Leadership effectiveness in global virtual teams. *Journal of Management Information Systems, 18*(3), 7–40.

Kirkman, B. L., & Mathieu, J. E. (2005). The dimensions and antecedents of team virtuality. *Journal of Management, 31*(5), 700–718.

Kirkman, B. L., Rosen, B., Tesluk, P. E., & Gibson, C. B. (2004). The impact of team empowerment on virtual team performance: The moderating role of face-to-face interaction. *Academy of Management Journal*, 18.

Kirkman, B., & Shapiro, D. (2005). The Impact of Cultural Value Diversity on Multicultural Team Performance☆. In *Advances in International Management* (Vol. 18, pp. 33–67). Elsevier.

Klimoski, R., & Mohammed, S. (1994). Team mental model: Construct or metaphor? *Journal of Management, 20*(2), 403–437.

Klitmøller, A., & Lauring, J. (2013). When global virtual teams share knowledge: Media richness, cultural difference and language commonality. *Journal of World Business, 48*(3), 398–406.

Kniffin, K. M., Narayanan, J., Anseel, F., Antonakis, J., Ashford, S. P., Bakker, A. B., Bamberger, P., Bapuji, H., Bhave, D. P., & Choi, V. K. (2021). COVID-19 and the workplace:

Implications, issues, and insights for future research and action. *American Psychologist, 76*(1), 63.

Köppel, P. (2007). *Konflikte und Synergien in multikulturellen Teams: Virtuelle und face-to-face-Kooperation*. Wiesbaden. Springer-Verlag.

Korsgaard, M. A., Brower, H. H., & Lester, S. W. (2015). It isn't always mutual: A critical review of dyadic trust. *Journal of Management, 41*(1), 47–70.

Kossek, E. E., & Lautsch, B. A. (2018). Work–life flexibility for whom? Occupational status and work–life inequality in upper, middle, and lower level jobs. *Academy of Management Annals, 12*(1), 5–36.

Kotlarsky, J., & Oshri, I. (2005). Social ties, knowledge sharing and successful collaboration in globally distributed system development projects. *European Journal of Information Systems, 14*(1), 37–48.

Kozlowski, S. W. J., & Ilgen, D. R. (2006). Enhancing the Effectiveness of Work Groups and Teams. *Psychological Science in the Public Interest, 7*(3), 77–124.

Kraut, R. E., Fussell, S. R., Brennan, S. E., & Siegel, J. (2002). Understanding effects of proximity on collaboration: Implications for technologies to support remote collaborative work. In *Distributed work* (pp. 137–162).

Kreps, D. M. (1990). Corporate culture and economic theory. In J. E. Alt & K. A. Shepsle (Eds.), *Perspectives on Positive Political Economy* (1st ed., pp. 90–143). Cambridge University Press.

Lectica, A. (2022). *Lectica Institute*. https://lecticalive.org/

Legifrance. (2022). *Déclaration des Droits de l'Homme et du Citoyen de 1789—Légifrance*. https://www.legifrance.gouv.fr/contenu/menu/droit-national-en-vigueur/constitution/declaration-des-droits-de-l-homme-et-du-citoyen-de-1789

Lewicki, R. J., & Brinsfield, C. (2017). Trust repair. *Annual Review of Organizational Psychology and Organizational Behavior, 4*, 287–313.

Lewis, J. D., & Weigert, A. (1985). Trust as a social reality. *Social Forces, 63*(4), 967–985.

Lipnack, J., & Stamps, J. (1999). Virtual teams: The new way to work. *Strategy & Leadership*.

Ma, J., Schaubroeck, J. M., & LeBlanc, C. (2019, March 26). *Interpersonal Trust in Organizations*. Oxford Research Encyclopedia of Business and Management.

Marks, M. A., Mathieu, J. E., & Zaccaro, S. J. (2001). A temporally based framework and taxonomy of team processes. *Academy of Management Review, 26*(3), 356–376.

Marlow, S. L., Lacerenza, C. N., & Salas, E. (2017). Communication in virtual teams: A conceptual framework and research agenda. *Human Resource Management Review, 27*(4), 575–589.

Maruping, L. M., & Agarwal, R. (2004). Managing team interpersonal processes through technology: A task-technology fit perspective. *Journal of Applied Psychology, 89*(6), 975–990.

Mathieu, J. E., Heffner, T. S., Goodwin, G. F., Salas, E., & Cannon-Bowers, J. A. (2000). The influence of shared mental models on team process and performance. *Journal of Applied Psychology, 85*(2), 273.

Mayer, R. C., Davis, J. H., & Schoorman, F. D. (1995). An integrative model of organizational trust. *Academy of Management Review, 20*(3), 709–734.

Maynard, M. T., & Gilson, L. L. (2014). The role of shared mental model development in understanding virtual team effectiveness. *Group & Organization Management, 39*(1), 3–32.

Maznevski, M. L., & Chudoba, K. M. (2000). Bridging space over time: Global virtual team dynamics and effectiveness. *Organization Science, 11*(5), 473–492.

McNamara, K., Dennis, A., & Carte, T. (2008). It's the Thought that Counts: The Mediating Effects of Information Processing in Virtual Team Decision Making. *Information Systems Management—ISM, 25*, 20–32.

Meluso, J., Johnson, S., & Bagrow, J. (2020). *Flexible Environments for Hybrid Collaboration: Redesigning Virtual Work Through the Four Orders of Design.*

Merriman, K. K., Schmidt, S. M., & Dunlap-Hinkler, D. (2007). Profiling virtual employees: The impact of managing virtually. *Journal of Leadership & Organizational Studies, 14*(1), 6–15.

Miller, C. (2003). Social psychology and virtue ethics. *The Journal of Ethics, 7*(4), 365–392.

Milliken, F. J., & Martins, L. L. (1996). Searching for Common Threads: Understanding the Multiple Effects of Diversity in Organizational Groups. *The Academy of Management Review, 21*(2), 402.

Montoya, M. M., Massey, A. P., Hung, Y. C., & Crisp, C. B. (2009). Can you hear me now? Communication in virtual product development teams. *Journal of Product Innovation Management, 26*(2), 139–155.

Morrison-Smith, S., & Ruiz, J. (2020). Challenges and barriers in virtual teams: A literature review. *SN Applied Sciences, 2*(6), 1–33.

Mortensen, M. (2014). Constructing the team: The antecedents and effects of membership model divergence. *Organization Science, 25*(3), 909–931.

Mortensen, M., & Hinds, P. J. (2001). Conflict and shared identity in geographically distributed teams. *International Journal of Conflict Management, 12*(3), 212–238.

Murthy, D., Rodriguez, A., & Lewis, J. (2013). *Examining the formation of swift trust within a scientific global virtual team.* 353–362.

Neusner, J., & Chilton, B. D. (2008). *The golden rule: The ethics of reciprocity in world religions.* Bloomsbury Publishing.

Nikolova, N., Möllering, G., & Reihlen, M. (2015). Trusting as a 'leap of faith': Trust-building practices in client–consultant relationships. *Scandinavian Journal of Management, 31*(2), 232–245.

Norman, S. M., Avey, J., Larson, M., & Hughes, L. (2019). The development of trust in virtual leader–follower relationships. *Qualitative Research in Organizations and Management: An International Journal, 15*(3), 279–295.

Northouse, P. (2013). *Leadership: Theory and Practice* (6th ed.). Thousand Oaks, CA Sage Publications.

Nydegger, R., & Nydegger, L. (2010). Challenges In Managing Virtual Teams. *Journal of Business & Economics Research (JBER), 8*(3), Article 3.

O'Leary & Cummings. (2007). The Spatial, Temporal, and Configurational Characteristics of Geographic Dispersion in Teams. *MIS Quarterly, 31*(3), 433.

O'Leary, M. B., & Mortensen, M. (2010). Go (Con)figure: Subgroups, Imbalance, and Isolates in Geographically Dispersed Teams. *Organization Science, 21*(1), 115–131.

Olson, G. M., & Olson, J. S. (2000). Distance matters. *Human-Computer Interaction, 15*(2), 139–178.

Olson, J., & Olson, G. (2006). Bridging Distance: Empirical Studies of Distributed Teams. *Human-Computer Interaction and Management Information Systems: Application 6*, 101.

Olson, J., & Olson, G. (2011). *Bridging Distance: Empirical Studies of Distributed Teams.*

Parker, S. K., Knight, C., & Keller, A. (2020). *Remote Managers Are Having Trust Issues.* https://hbr.org/2020/07/remote-managers-are-having-trust-issues

Peñarroja, V., Orengo, V., Zornoza, A., & Hernández, A. (2013). The effects of virtuality level on task-related collaborative behaviors: The mediating role of team trust. *Computers in Human Behavior*, *29*(3), 967–974.

Powers, T. (2018). *Virtual Teams For Dummies.* London. John Wiley & Sons.

Purvanova, R. K., & Bono, J. E. (2009). Transformational leadership in context: Face-to-face and virtual teams. *The Leadership Quarterly*, *20*(3), 343–357.

Resick, C. J., Dickson, M. W., Mitchelson, J. K., Allison, L. K., & Clark, M. A. (2010). Team composition, cognition, and effectiveness: Examining mental model similarity and accuracy. *Group Dynamics: Theory, Research, and Practice*, *14*(2), 174.

Resick, C. J., Murase, T., Bedwell, W. L., Sanz, E., Jiménez, M., & DeChurch, L. A. (2010). Mental model metrics and team adaptability: A multi-facet multi-method examination. *Group Dynamics: Theory, Research, and Practice*, *14*(4), 332.

Ring, P. S., & Van de Ven, A. H. (1994). Developmental processes of cooperative interorganizational relationships. *Academy of Management Review*, *19*(1), 90–118.

Robert Jr, L. P., & You, S. (2018). Are you satisfied yet? Shared leadership, individual trust, autonomy, and satisfaction in virtual teams. *Journal of the Association for Information Science and Technology*, *69*(4), 503–513.

Robert, L. P., Denis, A. R., & Hung, Y.-T. C. (2009). Individual swift trust and knowledge-based trust in face-to-face and virtual team members. *Journal of Management Information Systems*, *26*(2), 241–279.

Rosado, C. (1996). Toward a definition of multiculturalism. *Retrieved From.*

Rousseau, D. M., Sitkin, S. B., Burt, R. S., & Camerer, C. (1998). Not so different after all: A cross-discipline view of trust. *Academy of Management Review*, *23*(3), 393–404.

Sarker, S., Ahuja, M., Sarker, S., & Kirkeby, S. (2011). The Role of Communication and Trust in Global Virtual Teams: A Social Network Perspective. *Journal of Management Information Systems*, *28*(1), 273–310.

Saunders, C., Van Slyke, C., & Vogel, D. R. (2004). My time or yours? Managing time visions in global virtual teams. *Academy of Management Perspectives*, *18*(1), 19–37.

Schelling, T. C. (1980). *The Strategy of Conflict: With a new Preface by the Author*. Harvard university press.

Schmidtke, J. M., & Cummings, A. (2017). The effects of virtualness on teamwork behavioral components: The role of shared mental models. *Human Resource Management Review*, *27*(4), 660–677.

Scott, C. P., & Wildman, J. L. (2015). Culture, communication, and conflict: A review of the global virtual team literature. *Leading Global Teams*, 13–32.

Siebdrat, F., Hoegl, M., & Ernst, H. (2009). How to manage virtual teams. *MIT Sloan Management Review*, *50*(4), 63.

Singer, M. G. (1963). The Golden Rule. *Philosophy, Cambridge University Press*, *38*(146), 293–314.

Solomon, R. C. (1992). *Ethics and Excellence: Cooperation and Integrity in Business.* Oxford University Press.

Staples, D. S., & Zhao, L. (2006). The effects of cultural diversity in virtual teams versus face-to-face teams. *Group Decision and Negotiation*, *15*(4), 389–406.

Suchanek, A. (2007). *Ökonomische Ethik.* Mohr Siebeck Tübingen.

Suchanek, A. (2008). Business ethics and the golden rule. *Diskussionspapier Des Wittenberg-Zentrums Für Globale Ethik, 2003.*

Suchanek, A. (2013). Führungsethik. In *Handbuch Strategisches Personalmanagement* (pp. 333–345). Wiesbaden. Springer.

Suchanek, A. (2015). *Unternehmensethik: In Vertrauen investieren.* Mohr Siebeck.

Suchanek, A. (2017). Corporate Responsibility as the Avoidance of Relevant Inconsistencies. In R. R. Sharma, M. Csuri, & K. Ogunyemi (Eds.), *Managing for Responsibility: A Sourcebook for an Alternative Paradigm* (pp. 77–89). New York: Business Expert Press.

Suchanek, A. (2019a). *GUTE FÜHRUNG—BETRACHTUNGEN EINES UNTERNEHMENSETHIKERS.*

Suchanek, A. (2019b). *The Problem of Corporate Legitimacy. In J. D. Rendtorff (Ed.), Handbook of Business Legitimacy: Responsibility, Ethics and Society (pp. 1–22).* Springer International Publishing.

Suchanek, A. (2020). Kooperation. In L. Heidbrink, A. Lorch, & V. Rauen (Eds.), *Praktische Wirtschaftsphilosophie* (pp. 1–14). Springer Fachmedien Wiesbaden.

Suchanek, A., & Entschew, E. M. (2018). Ethical focal points as a complement to accelerated social change. *Humanistic Management Journal, 3*(2), 221–232.

Suchanek, A., & von Broock, M. (2008). Wertemanagement und Konsistenz. In *Wertemenagement und Wertschöpfung in Unter- nehmen. Fallstudien international erfolgreicher Unternehmen,* (p. S.17–54). Bertelsmann-Stiftung (Hrsg.):

Suchanek, A., & von Broock, M. (2009). Investitionen in den Faktor Vertrauen. *Hg. v. Wittenberg-Zentrum Für Globale Ethik e. V., Wittenberg (Diskussionspapier, 2009–3). . de/Urn: Nbn: De: Gbv, 3,* 2–10456.

Suchman, M. C. (1995). Managing Legitimacy: Strategic and Institutional Approaches. *Academy of Management Review, 20*(3), 571–610.

Suurendonk, M. (2017). *Metaphysics of Trust: A Propaedeutic* [Doctoral Dissertation, HHL Leipzig Graduate School of Management].

Swigger, K., Alpaslan, F., Brazile, R., & Monticino, M. (2004). Effects of culture on computer-supported international collaborations. *International Journal of Human-Computer Studies, 60*(3), 365–380.

Think-it. (2022). *Homepage.* Think-It. https://www.think-it.io/

Townsend, A. M., DeMarie, S. M., & Hendrickson, A. R. (1998). Virtual teams: Technology and the workplace of the future. *Academy of Management Perspectives, 12*(3), 17–29.

Treinen, J. J., & Miller-Frost, S. L. (2006). Following the sun: Case studies in global software development. *IBM Systems Journal, 45*(4), 773–783.

Trevino, L. K., Daft, R., & Lengel, R. (1990). 4. Understanding Managers' Media Choices: A Symbolic Interactionist. *Organizations and Communication Technology, 71.*

Triandis, H. C., & Gelfand, M. J. (1998). Converging measurement of horizontal and vertical individualism and collectivism. *Journal of Personality and Social Psychology, 74*(1), 118.

Wahren, H.-K. E. (1994). *Gruppen- und Teamarbeit in Unternehmen:* DE GRUYTER.

Walls, M. (2013). Sociocultural Differences. In M. D. Gellman & J. R. Turner (Eds.), *Encyclopedia of Behavioral Medicine* (pp. 1851–1851). Springer New York.

Walsh, J. P., & Maloney, N. G. (2007). Collaboration structure, communication media, and problems in scientific work teams. *Journal of Computer-Mediated Communication, 12*(2), 712–732.

Wang, B., Liu, Y., Qian, J., & Parker, S. K. (2021). Achieving Effective Remote Working During the COVID-19 Pandemic: A Work Design Perspective. *Applied Psychology, 70*(1), 16–59.

Warkentin, M., Sayeed, L., & Hightower, R. (1997). Virtual teams versus face-to-face teams. *Emerging Information Technologies: Improving Decisions, Cooperation, and Infrastructure*, 241–262.

Wattles, J. (1996). *The Golden Rule.* Oxford University Press.

WCGE. (2017). *An Ethical Compass for Good Leadership.* https://www.wcge.org/images/wissenschaft/doktorandenkolleg/dokumente/Suchanek_Ethical_Compass.pdf

Wilson, J. M., Boyer O'Leary, M., Metiu, A., & Jett, Q. R. (2008). Perceived proximity in virtual work: Explaining the paradox of far-but-close. *Organization Studies, 29*(7), 979–1002.

Wilson, J. M., Straus, S. G., & McEvily, B. (2006). All in due time: The development of trust in computer-mediated and face-to-face teams. *Organizational Behavior and Human Decision Processes, 99*(1), 16–33.

Yahaya, R., & Ebrahim, F. (2016). Leadership styles and organizational commitment: Literature review. *Journal of Management Development, 35*(2), 190–216.

Zaccaro, S. J., & Bader, P. (2003). E-leadership and the challenges of leading e-teams: Minimizing the bad and maximizing the good. *Organizational Dynamics.*

Zander, L., Zettinig, P., & Mäkelä, K. (2013). Leading global virtual teams to success. *Organizational Dynamics, 42*(3), 228–237.

Zigurs, I. (2003). Leadership in Virtual Teams: Oxymoron or Opportunity? *Organizational Dynamics, 31*(4), 339–351.

Zolin, R., Hinds, P. J., Fruchter, R., & Levitt, R. E. (2004). Interpersonal trust in cross-functional, geographically distributed work: A longitudinal study. *Information and Organization, 14*(1), 1–26.

MIX
Papier aus verantwortungsvollen Quellen
Paper from responsible sources
FSC® C105338

If you have any concerns about our products,
you can contact us on
ProductSafety@springernature.com

In case Publisher is established outside the EU,
the EU authorized representative is:
Springer Nature Customer Service Center GmbH
Europaplatz 3, 69115 Heidelberg, Germany

Printed by Libri Plureos GmbH
in Hamburg, Germany